AMERICAN HEROES

Also by Rick Leddy
LeBron James The King of the Game

Also by Noah Davis
The World's Best Soccer Strikers

*"Every time you fall down, it gives you an opportunity
to question yourself, question your integrity.
It's not about the actual failure itself—
it's how you respond to it."*
—ABBY WAMBACH

*"The harder you work and the more prepared you are
for something, you're going to be able
to persevere through anything."*
—CARLI LLOYD

AMERICAN HEROES

The U.S. Women's Soccer Team
Road to Glory

Noah Davis and Rick Leddy

Sole BOOKS

Editor: Y Ginsberg
Proof editor: Michele Caterina
Cover design: Omer Pikarsky
Front cover: Alex Morgan: REUTERS/Jose Manuel Ribeiro
             Hope Solo: REUTERS/Brian Snyder
             Carly Lloyd: Anne-Marie Sorvin-*USA TODAY* Sports
             Abby Wambach: Michael Chow-*USA TODAY* Sports
             Mia Hamm: Reuters photographer
Back cover: U.S team: Anne-Marie Sorvin-*USA TODAY* Sports
Inside page layout: Lynn Snyder

Library of Congress Cataloging-in-Publication data available.

ISBN: 978-1-938591-36-5

Copyright © 2015 by Sole Books Beverly Hills. All rights reserved.

Published by Sole Books, Beverly Hills, California

Printed in the United States of America

First edition September 2015

10987654321

www.solebooks.com

1

As soon as she turned, Carli Lloyd knew what to do. It was the same thing she'd done so many times during her soccer career; an action she practiced over and over again. It was something she had worked on just in case the right moment presented itself in a match. And this was the right moment. On the field at BC Place in Vancouver, Canada, Carli Lloyd knew what she needed to do.

Shoot!

In the stadium, 53,341 people were watching the 2015 Women's World Cup final between the USA and Japan. Most were dressed in the red, white, and blue of the United States. Millions more were watching the game on television.

Lloyd took a touch that brought the ball just over the halfway line, more than fifty yards from the Japanese goal. Then she blasted a shot with her powerful right foot. It arched gracefully over the pitch toward the Japanese net. The noisy crowd was momentarily stunned by the audacity of the midfielder's attempt. What was she thinking? Did she really just try that? And was it really on target?

Lloyd was the unsung hero of the American team who had lifted the U.S. in the quarterfinals against China and in the semifinals against number-one-ranked Germany. She had already scored two goals in the final that helped the U.S. jump to a commanding 3-0 lead just 15 minutes into the match.

But a shell-shocked Japanese team that had given up three goals in quick succession wasn't expecting this. Ayumi Kaihori, the Japanese goalkeeper, seemed most surprised of all. Off her line near the top of the penalty area, she retreated back to her goal as fast as she could after the ball left Lloyd's foot. Falling backwards at the six-yard box, she reached skyward, trying to keep the ball out of the net and managed to tip it with the end of her gloved fingers. It altered the course of the ball, but not enough. Lloyd's screamer bounced off the inside of the left post and into the back of the net.

Just like that, Lloyd had her hat trick, the fastest in Women's World Cup history, and the Stars and Stripes had a huge 4-0 lead. A little more than an hour of playing time later, they were lifting the World Cup trophy after a lopsided 5-2 victory.

"We just wrote history today," Lloyd said after the game.

And she was right. Medals, trophies, and winning are a common theme for the U.S. Women's soccer team. Since the team debuted in its first game at the Mundialito (Little World Cup) tournament in 1985, the American women have been one of the world's best sides. The team, ranked No. 1 in the world for most of the past two-and-a-half decades, has featured famous faces such as Mia Hamm—the planet's long-time, all-time leading goal scorer—and Abby Wambach, the Pittsford, New York-born striker who broke Hamm's record of 158 international goals.

The women won the World Cup in 1991, 1999, and again in 2015, becoming the first nation to hoist the trophy three times. Their dramatic second victory made the cover of *Sports Illustrated* with Brandi Chastain, who scored the winning penalty kick against China, on her knees, jersey off, screaming in celebration, fists balled in triumph. The Americans also boast three Olympic gold medals, having won in 1996, 2008, and 2012.

The sustained success of the program is evident. Every coach who has led the team for more than five games can boast they have won at least 70 percent of their matches while helming Team U.S.A. Pia Sundhage, the former Swedish star who led the U.S. to two Olympic gold medals, won nine out of every 10 games. Throughout the history of women's soccer, American stars from Mia Hamm and Chastain to Abby Wambach, Lloyd, and Alex Morgan, have been consistently and undeniably the world's best.

But in the beginning of 2015, the U.S. team found itself at a crossroads. Going into the tournament, they weren't ranked No. 1. The rest of the world had caught up and countries like Japan, Germany, France, and Sweden were level with the Americans in terms of skill. The wonderful gold medal run in the London Olympics had been impressive but also somewhat lucky. Team

U.S.A. was often forced to rely upon hard work and physical superiority rather than tactics and talent. Gone were the days when the U.S. could show up on the pitch and presume to win. The world of women's soccer had changed, and the Americans were suddenly fighting to remain on top. They had plenty of young, talented players like Tobin Heath, Sydney Leroux, Christian Press, and Morgan Brian in addition to Alex Morgan; but it was their new manager Jill Ellis' job to develop the youngsters while keeping the old guard sharp and winning games.

At the beginning of 2015 there were voices who doubted the Americans. Could they find a way to win the tournament? Could they integrate the older players with the new? Could they improve and take home a trophy that had eluded them for 16 years?

This is the story of the U.S. Women's National Team, the good, the bad, and the ugly; the past, the present, and the future. Come along for the ride; it's a tale filled with soaring wins, crushing losses, trophies, gold medals, and a few songs along the way.

2

For all the success the American women would find, the journey began slowly. In 1985, Dublin, Ireland-born Mike Ryan, who had briefly played soccer professionally as a young man in England before emigrating to the United States in the 1950s, oversaw a four-team tournament at the Olympic Sports Festival in Baton Rouge, Louisiana. Nearly 70 women, the best players in the country, participated. At the conclusion of the event, Ryan, who had been picked to coach a squad that would represent the United States at the Mundialito tournament in Italy, picked 17 women for his roster.

And thus, the first U.S. Women's National Team was born.

This hastily put together hodgepodge of young soccer talent from across the nation included women who played for varsity college teams and independent club teams. In 1985, only 201 colleges across the United States supported women's varsity soccer squads, compared to 521 for men.

But things were changing in the United States and the popularity of soccer was growing among women and girls. Youth programs such as the American Youth Soccer Organization (AYSO) gave young girls a chance to hone their skills and the participation of women at the high school and college level was soaring. Suddenly, the United States was bursting to the seams with young women who were falling in love with the beautiful game.

With the popularity of women's soccer exploding in the States and a timely invitation from the Italian Soccer Federation that offered to pay for part of the U.S. team's airfare, it seemed like the right moment for the United States to take a leap on to the international stage. Ready or not.

But it was a humble beginning.

The newly formed team had exactly three practices

together before they were scheduled to fly to Italy
to play against far more experienced and seasoned
European sides. At the last-minute, they were issued
men's soccer uniforms and the new teammates had
to hastily sew the letters "USA" onto their shorts
at a local sporting goods store the day before they
departed for the tournament. In this seat-of-your-pants
environment, the fledgling squad bonded. After all,
they were going to play the game they loved against stiff
international competition and were getting $10 a day
for meals to do it!

Mike Ryan named Denise Bender team captain.
She was a tough and talkative back line defender
who had played for him on a Seattle-based club team.
She was ready and confident to lead the inaugural
U.S. Women's National team into its first international
match, and was amazed by the enthusiastic response
women's soccer received in Italy. Women playing in the
States were used to playing before small crowds
and empty stadium seats, but here 10,000 fans packed
the stadium for their first game of the tournament in
Jesolo, Italy, on August 18, 1985. They were playing
against the mighty and talented home country

favorites—the Italian National Team.

Despite the Americans being the visiting team, the Italians took a liking to the young and spunky squad and began chanting in unison, "Ooosa, Ooosa, Ooosa!," which was their version of "USA, USA, USA."

The American team adopted the chant and they still use it today.

While the Italian home crowd supported the young visitors, the result didn't go their way. Italy—bigger, faster, and stronger—scored first, but the Red, White, and Blue continued fighting. Eight minutes from the end of the match, they earned a chance to tie after Cindy Gordon was taken down in the box. A penalty kick! Sharon McMurty, the U.S. Soccer Player of the Year for 1985, stepped to the spot. The crowd hushed as she looked at the Italian goalkeeper and then ran towards the ball. She sent it flying goalward in search of the first American women's team goal ever. But it was not to be. Her attempt missed to the left. The U.S. ended their first international game with a 1-0 loss.

"Penalty kicks always made me nervous," McNulty said, "In that kind of a game, I was extremely nervous."

But the American squad had learned some valuable

lessons. Bender remembered that the Italians played a different game than the members of the youthful American team had experienced before. She was impressed by their "drama" but not so much by their "sneaky activities."

Most of all, though, she was impressed by the support of the fans.

"They were chanting for us. Kids were there after the games for autographs. That stuff was totally new to me," Bender said.

The Americans went into their second game of the tournament against Denmark with a new confidence. The crowd had been behind them during their first match and they had held their own against a very good and physical Italian team.

And arguably the best player on their squad had not even seen action in their first match.

Center forward, Michelle Akers, had been sidelined with an ankle injury. She was an All-American high school and college player who had a nose for the goal and who, at 5'10" and 150 pounds, was a force to be reckoned with. Although born in Santa Clara, California, she mostly grew up in the Seattle,

Washington, area, where she honed some of her hard-nosed skills playing on the high school men's varsity soccer team.

The Americans would need all the ammunition they could get to battle a very tough and very talented Danish National Team.

Michelle Akers and Emily Pickering, who had also missed the first match due to injury, did the attacking work. Akers scored the first-ever goal in U.S. Women's National Team history on an assist by Pickering, putting the U.S. up 1-0. The Danes later leveled the score, but then Pickering found the back of the net, scoring on a beautiful, curling left-footed shot that found the upper side of the net.

The quick and experienced Danish team leveled the score near the end of the match and it ended in a 2-2 draw. However, it had been a day of firsts for the young Americans. They had scored their first goals in an international tournament, had experienced their first lead, and had fought to their first draw against a quality opponent.

It was heady stuff for a group of athletes, many who had never been overseas, to stand toe-to-toe and tie a strong international competitor.

As the tournament wore on, the U.S. would fall to England, 3-1, with Akers getting her second international goal in that match. The team would then go on to lose to Denmark, 1-0, in a consolation battle.

Although the U.S. finished the "Little World Cup" without a victory, they had made some important and vital first steps and had gained some valuable experience. And the first of a long line of American women soccer stars had been introduced to the world. Michelle Akers was just beginning an amazing career that would later result in her being named the FIFA Women's World Player of the Century.

That first American squad returned home to the States with their heads held high. The future was bright.

And then the team disbanded.

Having accomplished their goal of playing against international competitors in Italy, the players on the first women's team went their separate ways to rejoin club teams or university programs. Without a strong formal organization, the team was essentially a pickup team made up of some of the finest players in the country.

When the United States was invited again to the Mundialito in 1986, it was much the same situation except that Mike Ryan was out as coach, in favor of the fiery and competitive Anson Dorrance.

The University of North Carolina (UNC) coach was the son of an American oil executive who had to travel for business. He was born in India and lived in Kenya, Ethiopia, Belgium, Singapore, and Switzerland as a child. It was in Ethiopia where he was first exposed to soccer. As a youth, Dorrance had a reputation for intensity on the pitch and in the classroom. He brought that same drive with him as a walk-on soccer player at UNC and then later as head coach of the men's and the women's soccer teams at the university.

Dorrance had wanted to be the first coach of the National Team, but had lost the job to Ryan. The United States Soccer Federation (USSF) decided to give him a chance to helm the 1986 team because of his reputation as a winner at the college level. When he got the job he promised, "I am going to win."

That was certainly the case at University of North Carolina, where Dorrance had built the women's program from the ground up and had molded the Lady

Tar Heels into a dominating soccer powerhouse.

He immediately put the Women's National Team on notice. In a letter he sent to the players after he was given the head coach nod, he stated, "If you don't come to training camp fit, I will cut you!" He believed that only a physically fit team could be a winning team and the training regimen he put his teams through was notoriously tough.

True to his word, the U.S. team won its first match under his watch. On July 7, 1986, the Americans lined up against Canada's National Team at the Blaine Soccer Complex in Minnesota. Akers didn't play, but holdovers from the first national team including goalkeeper Kim Wyant, defender Lori Henty, and Pickering suited up. April Heinrichs, a brilliant, hard-headed, 22-year-old striker, who would later become team captain, made her debut. In a hard-fought match, the Americans prevailed 2-0. Two days later, they defeated the Canadians once again 3-0 to claim the inaugural North American Championship.

Dorrance had the first of his many trophies.

Back in the 1986 Mundialito in Italy, the U.S. fared much better than the previous year, defeating China,

Brazil, and Japan, before falling to the Italians for a second-place finish in the tournament.

It appeared that Dorrance's philosophy of fitness and competitiveness was working. But he also had an eye on the future of the program, and that future included a teenage soccer phenomenon named Mariel Margaret Hamm.

People simply called her Mia.

Dorrance was looking for soccer talent, no matter what the player's age or size. He first heard of Hamm when a friend told him he needed to come to a youth tournament in North Texas to see a skinny, 14-year-old kid play. Dorrance was immediately impressed by the speed of the youngster. When he first saw her make a run with the ball, it looked like she had been "shot out of a cannon." He got up immediately, having seen all he needed to see and said to himself, "Oh my gosh."

What happened next was a whirlwind for Hamm. Dorrance talked with her coaches about her potential and suddenly she found herself training with the Women's National Team. Dorrance told her if she worked hard, she could become a great player.

Hamm felt as if her head was spinning. She was

only 15 when she made her debut on the national team in 1987.

But Dorrance wasn't finished with his hunt for youthful soccer talent. Future stars Kristine Lilly and Julie Foudy were only 16 when they were recruited for the national team. Joy Beifeld (later Joy Fawcett) and Brandi Chastain were 19 when they got the call.

It was all a bit overwhelming and intimidating for a group of teenagers suddenly thrust into the elite circle of women's soccer in the United States. Michelle Akers called them "kids"— and they were, compared to the veterans on the squad who were in their mid-twenties. It was a confusing and thrilling time for these future soccer stars.

Fawcett didn't even know there was a Women's National Team until she got to the training camp. When Lilly first arrived at training camp, a young man who she did not recognize said hello to her. Baffled, she asked fellow teammate Hamm who had just greeted her.

"That's Anson," Hamm replied. "The coach."

Dorrance's move towards youth from 1987 to 1990 was not popular in some U.S. soccer circles. But he felt that this was the core to the future of the Women's National Team. It proved extremely unpopular when he cut several senior members of the team to make room for the youthful "Fab 5" of Hamm, Chastain, Lilly, Foudy, and Fawcett. Dorrance was put on notice by senior administrators of the United States Soccer Federation that if his gamble on youth didn't work out, his job was on the line. Despite the pressure, Dorrance was convinced that the future of the national team lay with a roster made up of experienced veterans like Akers and Heinrichs and the "kids" who were willing to train hard and do what it took to win.

On August 3, 1987, Hamm, Lilly and Fawcett, made their first appearances for the Stars and Stripes during a 2-0 win over The People's Republic of China. The "kids" continued to push themselves to get better, both on the national team and at universities around the country. Hamm and Lilly went on to play for Dorrance at the University of North Carolina, while Fawcett, Chastain, and Foudy honed their skills at schools in California. These youthful members were proving the doubters wrong and they were getting stronger and more skilled each year. It looked like Dorrance had been right in sticking to his guns by recruiting and keeping these young and talented women on the squad. The team was improving rapidly.

But how good were they?

The U.S. squad was about to find out at the first Women's World Championship.

3

Michelle Akers could not believe her luck.

Nearly 65,000 fans at Tianhe Stadium in Guangzhou, China, held their collective breath as Akers pounced on a poor back pass from Norwegian defender Tina Svensson to goalkeeper Reidun Seth. It was an uncharacteristic mistake for Svensson, one of the best defenders in the world, but the relentless Akers, wearing a red knee brace, was ready to take advantage of the miscue. If she did, she would likely secure victory for the Americans. They would be champions, the first team ever to appear on FIFA's trophy. Could Akers find the back of the net with the ball like she had done so many times before?

Akers had already scored once against the tough and

formidable Norwegians in the final. But the score was even at 1-1. With time running out for both squads, she knew that if she buried this strike it would be her most important goal in the tournament and maybe ever. It would be the goal that could win it all for the United States, the goal that would prove that a squad assembled only five years earlier had become the best team in the world.

It was the chance at goal every striker dreams of. The goal she had thought about as a kid.

The road to Aker's "dream goal" attempt in the world championship final began earlier in April when the American women traveled to Varna, Bulgaria, for friendly matches against Yugoslavia, Bulgaria, Hungary, France, and the USSR. They won all five matches easily, scoring 24 goals and giving up zero. Mia Hamm had just turned 19 in March and took off the 1991 season from UNC to focus on the World Championship. Hamm and Kristine Lilly, another UNC player, fresh off winning the Hermann Trophy as the college game's best player, starred in supporting roles, while Akers scored eight goals in those games.

The Americans, quite simply, were making it look easy. Coach Dorrance's insistence that his squad be the most physically fit team in the world was paying off. They spent hours sprinting and doing distance running. The hard work had two effects: it increased the team's fitness and it brought them together as a team. They bonded with each other as they met the nearly impossible standards the coach set.

"We were playing a game that we truly enjoyed and loved and we were playing with people we cared so much about," central defender Carla Overbeck said. "We didn't care where we went, as long as we were together and playing soccer."

The winner of the eight-team Confederation of North, Central American, and Caribbean Association Football (CONCACAF) championship contested in Port-au-Prince, Haiti would be the only squad to qualify for the Women's World Championship later that year in China, so there was no room for failure.

The American women didn't leave anything to chance, establishing their dominance over the inferior competition from the outset. A 12-0 drubbing of Mexico, featuring five goals from substitute Brandi

Chastain, was followed by lopsided scores of 12-0, 10-0, and 10-0. Only Canada managed to keep the powerful U.S. from reaching double digits, losing 5-0 in the final. After five victories—49 goals for and zero against— Anson Dorrance's women were going to the Far East.

Before the trip, the team sat in New York's JFK Airport alone, each woman alone with her thoughts. Hamm tried on her new jersey, while Akers washed down a Taco Bell snack with frozen yogurt from TCBY.

Despite the Americans' impressive string of victories and their being one of the most dominant teams in the world, their trip to compete in the very first women's championship in China got little attention from the media. Most American sports journalists didn't understand, nor care much about, the world's most popular sport.

"Nobody in the States really had a clue," Julie Foudy said. "They would ask us things like, 'Is the World Cup co-ed? How do you do it? How does it work?' Nobody had any idea."

Even FIFA showed the women little respect. The federation had considered making the women play with a youth-sized #4 ball instead of the adult #5. They shortened the women's games from 90 minutes to 80 minutes, figuring that playing a full 90 minutes might prove too strenuous for women. It was a move that had to have made the American women laugh after surviving Anson Dorrance's grueling training regimen.

Finally, FIFA didn't even call the tournament the Women's World Cup. Although FIFA's name was attached to the tournament, it was a less than enthusiastic endorsement. The tournament was officially called the "FIFA Women's World Championship for the M&M's Cup." Basically, the cup was named for a candy made by the Mars candy company—the tournament's only official sponsor.

While the American public and FIFA were showing the tournament little love, the host, China made up for that.

When the team got to China, it seemed that the whole country was looking forward to the tournament. Michelle Akers was surprised. "They were excited about it ... It was a big deal... I was like 'Wow, what are all these people doing here?'"

Twelve teams from around the world had been invited to compete, but despite the Americans' domination in the matches leading up to their appearance, their victory at the World Championship was far from assured.

In warmup matches during August, September, and October, the U.S. played The People's Republic of China and Norway a total of seven times, winning just two and losing four. It was not the type of send-off the Americans anticipated, but Dorrance was testing his lineup and trying to find the best fit for his talented players. In Akers, with Carin Jennings (later Carin Gabarra), and team captain April Heinrichs, he had one of the best attacking trios on the planet. They were nicknamed "The Triple-Edge Sword." The three women intuitively understood where the other two would be on the field. But still, the U.S. was not the favorite when they traveled to China in the fall of 1991.

"We were so nervous," Julie Foudy said, "We were scared to play China, we were scared to play Japan. We were just spazzing out."

The team was also scared of something else: the food in China. They had played in China before and many on the team had experienced stomach problems from the local food they ate. It got so bad that, according to

Foudy, whenever the team traveled to China to play, their meals consisted of peanut butter sandwiches, Snickers, and warm Pepsi.

Dorrance decided that this "breakfast of champions" was not exactly what he wanted his team to survive on during a championship run. He asked his brother, Pete, and another friend, who were both in the restaurant business in Chapel Hill, North Carolina, if they would come along to cook homemade meals for the team.

Despite their concerns, the Americans easily dispatched their opponents in the group stage. Sweden fell 3-2, followed by Brazil (5-0) and Japan (3-0). After a quarterfinal destruction of Chinese Taipei 7-0, a game in which Michelle Akers scored 5 goals, the U.S. was to meet Germany in the semifinal.

But before that match, there was another important match to attend to—one back in North Carolina. The Lady Tar Heels were playing Wisconsin in the NCAA final, and nine members of Dorrance's team in China had attended, or were currently attending, UNC. Dorrance, who had left his assistant coach in charge so he could helm the national team in China, called home for updates during the game, which was not an easy task in a mostly pre-cell phone world. Hamm, Lilly, and seven other women waited nervously.

At the time, UNC was so deeply talented that it could lose its best players to the women's national team and still be competitive. In the end, UNC won 3-1. Nearly half of the U.S. squad celebrated another national championship for their college team.

After celebrating the Lady Tar Heels' victory, the American women set their sights on Germany. Before the game, Dorrance had them practice pantomime penalty kicks without the ball to help calm their nerves in case the game came down to penalty kicks. But that was unnecessary. Jennings netted a hat trick in the first 33 minutes with Heinrichs adding two more in a 5-2 rout.

Dorrance had high praise for Jennings: "She shreds defenses. She absolutely shreds them."

Only one more game remained: the final against Norway. Going into the tournament, the strong and physical Norwegian team was considered the team to beat for the championship. The Americans knew they would have a fight on their hands.

For much of the final game against Norway, it

appeared as though the Americans would lose. Although Akers scored first, tallying in the 20th minute, the Scandinavian team fought back. Linda Medalen evened the game just nine minutes later. The game was tied going into halftime.

After the break, Norway dominated possession. They passed around the bewildered Americans, who didn't have an answer. But the defense held on, bending but never breaking.

It was in the 78th minute that Akers got her chance to score the "goal you think about as a kid."

Akers intercepted Svensson's miscued back tap and then touched the ball around the Norwegian goalie, leaving her helplessly sprawled on the pitch. She suddenly found herself all alone in the six-yard box. History in the making was then a simple two-touch tap into the goal to give the U.S. a 2-1 lead with only two minutes remaining in the game.

The sold-out crowd of 65,000 erupted like a volcano.

For Anson Dorrance the last minutes of the match were the longest in his life. "Oh my gosh, we could win this thing. We could win this thing," he remembers thinking.

And when the final whistle finally blew, the Americans had won the first women's soccer world championship!

Goalkeeper Mary Harvey fell to her knees in relief while the rest of her teammates celebrated in the center of the pitch just outside the 18-yard box. The team raised the trophy high and Jennings won the first Golden Ball for being the tournament's most outstanding player.

On the bus ride back to the team hotel, the celebrating U.S. sang Queen's, "We Are the Champions," while hoisting the trophy among themselves.

Then they jumped on a plane and flew back to JFK Airport where they were sure throngs of fans were surely waiting to greet the new world champions. Brandi Chastain thought that this was the team that was going to change soccer in America. "People are now going to pay attention," she thought on the way back home.

But when they got back, three people were waiting for them at the airport. Three.

No screaming fans. No ticker tape parade. Nobody asking for autographs. For all they had accomplished, the Women's National Team had not captivated America. Interest in soccer in the U.S. was still dismal. It was obvious that America was not yet ready to embrace the beautiful game and that it was going to be an uphill battle to win the hearts and minds of the public—especially when it came to women's soccer.

April Heinrichs was philosophical about the lack of support. She said that it didn't matter what kind of reception they got when they got home. "I could care less how many people were waiting for us at the airport. It didn't diminish it... it was a world championship."

After bringing home the championship, it was clear that some things were going to change. Heinrichs, who tallied 36 goals in 46 international games, retired after the 1991 World Championship, and the "kids" were not so young anymore. They were poised to become the new leaders of an evolving women's national team. There was going to be a changing of the guard and two things were clear: the U.S. was now the defending world champions, and it was Hamm's team to lead.

4

Once again, the U.S. team disbanded after winning the world championship. The USSF had little money and seemingly little interest in keeping the team together, leaving many of the women wondering what would happen next. There were no practices planned for the future and they had no official facilities where they could train. Everything was on a wait-and-see basis.

While the younger members of the squad went back to play for college teams, many of the older women were left in a bind. They needed to find jobs to make ends meet. Unlike today, where players are paid to train and can pick up lucrative endorsement contracts, in 1991, soccer was still considered a hobby in the United States.

Despite the United States women's team being world champions, the future of the program was still very much in doubt.

Brandi Chastain left the team to play soccer professionally in Japan. She claims she never intended to retire from the team, but felt that she needed to seize the opportunity since there were no professional women's teams in the States. "In the back of my mind, I always wanted to return to the national team," she said.

Joy Fawcett faced a different problem. She wanted to have children and was confronted with the difficult choice of starting a family or staying with the team. It was a tough decision, because she loved playing soccer, but she chose to have children and left the national squad—but only temporarily, it turned out.

Meanwhile, veteran inspirational team leader Michelle Akers was fighting a different battle with an invisible foe. After the 1991 World Championship, she complained of feeling weak and exhausted. She just didn't feel right. When she trained, she would break out in sweats and would have no energy. Always an elite athlete, she couldn't understand why she was feeling so run down.

Doctors later diagnosed her with Chronic Fatigue Syndrome and told her there was no cure for it. They unhelpfully suggested that she would just have to learn to live with it and rest as much as possible. Being the keen competitor she was, she refused to surrender. She chose not to retire from the team, but as long as she continued to play soccer, she would always face two opponents: the one on the pitch and the one within her own body.

The "kids" were developing into stronger players at the college level. Mia Hamm and Kristine Lilly were both on the powerhouse University of North Carolina soccer team coached by Anson Dorrance, who was still officially the coach of the national team. It was clear that Dorrance had a future superstar in Mia Hamm.

Mia's mother had been a ballet dancer and had nicknamed her daughter after the famous prima ballerina, Mia Slavenska. But this Mia had no interest in becoming a dancer. She wanted to play sports.

She was quiet, but under that soft-spoken exterior was a fierce competitor. Born with a club foot that required a leg brace to correct, she credited her older brother, Garrett, whom she idolized, with getting her into sports. And she had plenty of competition growing up with four sisters and a brother.

"When I was a kid, I would quit a lot of games because I hated losing so much," she admitted. "I thought if I'd quit before the game was over then I really didn't lose."

That competitive nature didn't exactly endear her much with her siblings, as it wouldn't enamor her with the many opponents on the world stage who had the unenviable task of trying to stop her.

Somehow, Anson Dorrance had sensed the relentless competitor in the teenage Hamm that lay just below her calm surface. The girl who didn't like to talk about herself did all of her talking on the pitch. She was someone Dorrance would mold into an unstoppable force of nature as she led the Lady Tar Heels to four consecutive national titles. She was so good that she inherited the nickname "Jordan" while playing at UNC—after a certain basketball player who had once starred at UNC named Michael Jordan.

She was that good. And she was just getting started.

5

The national team didn't play much in 1992. In the two matches they did play, they lost to Norway: 3-1 and 4-2.

There was no love lost between the Norwegian squad and the Americans. The American team called their archrivals "the Vikings," because they were tall, athletic, and physical. Some of the members of Team U.S.A. had less flattering names for the Scandinavian team, but Kristine Lilly thought it was good for the team to have a healthy rivalry. Lilly was blunt when she spoke about the Norwegian team: "They were a team we just hated, and I'm sure that's what made it such a great rivalry, because I think they hated us, as well."

In 1993 the squad saw more action and a much

better winning percentage. They played 17 matches and won 13 of them.

A year later, Anson Dorrance stepped down as head coach of the national team, handing the reigns to Tony DiCicco, who had been the goalkeeper coach since 1991. The move surprised some, but Dorrance felt that the double-duty assignment of coaching the national team and UNC was taking a toll on the program he loved the most—UNC women's soccer. He believed the UNC women needed his full-time commitment if they were going to remain competitive in the college ranks.

That decision worked out well for UNC: to date Dorrance's teams have brought home 22 of 36 NCAA national championships, a record unmatched by any college coach in the nation. It is a legacy that led the UNC athletic department to officially declare him "a precious gem."

It seemed that DiCicco was up to the task of filling Dorrance's very big shoes, though. In 1994 the U.S. went 12 and 1 and qualified for the 1995 World Cup. This World Cup was going to be played in Sweden. FIFA had even officially embraced the women's game by designating the 1995 world championship the "FIFA Women's World Cup," as opposed to the "M&M's Cup."

This time, the women's team received a bit more attention before flying to Sweden to compete in the World Cup, but the crowds still weren't enormous. Before the team's flight left Chicago's O'Hare International Airport, U.S. Soccer Federation Executive Director Hank Steinbrecher was on hand to tell them, "You are the best of what we have to offer."

A varsity soccer team from a nearby high school also held up good luck signs. It wasn't an enormous send-off, but when compared to the attention the team had received before the 1991 tournament, it seemed like a ticker-tape parade.

The tournament promised to be the most difficult test the young American team had ever faced. They were the favorites entering the event, but Sweden, along with China, Norway, and Germany were still formidable opponents.

In the days before the start of the 1995 World Cup, the women tried to remain loose. They went to a local amusement park in their spare time and also played

Pictionary, charades, and pinochle. A day before the opening game, midfielders Julie Foudy and Tisha Venturini lined up half-filled water bottles in the hotel hall and played bowling with soccer balls.

But below this lighthearted surface there were some real concerns about Michelle Akers and her ability to compete in the tournament. Being the competitor she was, she refused to even think about not competing in the World Cup, despite her physical struggles with Chronic Fatigue Syndrome. There was still doubt among her teammates and coaches about whether she would be able to stand up to the rigorous physical demands of the World Cup tournament. The team had come to rely on Aker's leadership and goal scoring to carry them. Would she be able to hold up? If not, who would be able to inspire the team on to another World Cup championship?

When the first match against China began, Akers took the field despite her condition— but not for long. On a Chinese corner kick five minutes into the match, Akers was speared in the back of the head by a Chinese player going for a header. Immediately, Akers went down, unconscious on the field. She had to leave the game, having suffered a concussion and a knee injury. The match ended in a 3-3 draw and raised some real concerns as to the fate of the American team in the tournament. Akers was now out of group play, so the American squad looked to Lilly, Hamm, and Tisha Venturini to fill the huge hole left by her loss.

Ironically, the woman who would one day hold the record for the most goals scored in international competition was tapped to stop goals during the next match against Denmark. In the final minutes of that group game, goalkeeper Briana Scurry was sent off with a red card for the seemingly trivial offense of punting the ball slightly outside of the penalty box. Surprisingly, Mia Hamm got the nod to play in goal. Imagine that: one of the world's best strikers standing in goal! The versatile Hamm, who had earlier scored a goal in the game, also made a save!

The U.S. won 2-0 and then moved on to a quarterfinal victory against Japan.

That victory set up a semifinal World Cup rematch against the hated Norwegians. During group play, the once-favored Americans had taken a back seat to the Norwegian squad, which had breezed through their games. People were no longer betting that the Stars and Stripes would take it all.

Akers, despite a sore knee and a concussion, was not going to miss this rematch. Hobbled by injury and disease, she willed herself to be on the pitch to face "the Vikings" yet again. Seeing Akers on the pitch inspired Mia Hamm. She and the other players hoped that the veteran star would "carry us again… we expected Michelle to win the game for us."

But she couldn't. Norwegian Ann Kristin Aarønes, the tournament's top scorer, headed the ball into the back of the net from a corner kick in the 10th minute and that was all the Norwegians would need. The goal haunted goalkeeper Briana Scurry. "I missed it by an inch," she said, frustrated.

In the second half, the U.S. desperately threw everything they had at the Norwegians, but Norway held strong and, at the final whistle, the U.S. found themselves on the losing end of a 1-0 score against their archrivals. The name "United States" would not be etched on the 1995 Women's World Cup trophy.

After the match, the winners celebrated by joining hands to ankles and crawling around the field. They called it "The Train." U.S. team captain, Carla Overbeck, felt it was disrespectful and that Norway was "rubbing in" their victory over the United States. Michelle Akers said that it was all she could do to not go over to the Norwegians and "knock their heads off." It didn't help that one of the Norwegian players interviewed after the game said, "It's fun to beat the Americans because they get so upset and make so much noise when they lose. This is a problem. Never be weak."

What had been a heated rivalry now erupted into flames. The Americans vowed revenge.

Meanwhile, an ex-teammate was watching the game on television. She helplessly witnessed the heartbreak of her good friends and old teammates after the loss. She vowed right then that she would do whatever it took to find her way back to the team.

6

It was 1996 and the United States was set to host the Summer Olympics in Atlanta, Georgia. It was a huge opportunity for the national squad because, for the first time ever, women's soccer was going to be an event at the Summer Olympic Games. Not only would the team have an opportunity to win the inaugural event's first gold medal, but they would have the chance to do it at home. The media exposure that the U.S. team would get as a result could be huge for them and it could be even bigger for the future growth of soccer in America.

While next to nobody in the States had watched the Women's World Cup in 1995, the 1996 Summer Olympics would be a completely different story. It could change everything.

But it almost didn't happen.

Some of players on the women's team found out that the U.S. Soccer Federation was offering bonuses to the men's Olympic team if they won a Gold, Silver, or Bronze medal at the games. Which was fine, except that the federation was only offering the women's team a bonus if they brought home the Gold.

Many on the team thought that was unfair.

So, eight months before the Games were to begin, nine players, including Mia Hamm, Julie Foudy, Michelle Akers, Kristine Lilly, Briana Scurry, and team captain Carla Overbeck went on strike, refusing to go to the Olympic training camp until things had changed.

It was a scary proposition for those players. They really wanted to play in the Olympics before a home crowd. But they felt that if they didn't take a stand, the women's team would always be fighting for respect. Refusing to play was the only weapon they had at their disposal.

Suddenly there was a scramble to find players to replace the missing stars. That is when a certain ex-player who had vowed to find her way back to the national squad saw her opportunity. Just like that, Brandi Chastain was back on the team as a replacement player. If the striking players didn't like what she was doing, they never told Chastain. She felt that this was her only chance to get back with the national team. And when the dispute was finally settled a month later and the striking players came back, Chastain found she still had a spot on the team roster.

With the dispute over, it was time to get to business. DiCicco was still helming the team and was employing new methods, like hiring a sports psychologist, to train his player's minds as well as their bodies.

Although the Americans had the home field advantage with large supportive pro-American crowds cheering them on at the 1996 Olympic Games, it was not a given that they would win Gold. There had been no time to hold Olympic qualifying games, so the top eight finishers in the 1995 World Cup had been chosen to compete in the Olympics. That meant that the hated "Vikings" would once again be standing stoutly in the United States' path to Gold. They came into the Olympics ranked number one in the world and were favored to take it all. But the loss to the Norwegians at the World Cup still smoldered hot in the Americans' memory. A picture of the Norwegian team performing "The Train" after their victory over the U.S. in the World Cup hung prominently near the door in the team's training room. Some days after training the players punched the picture.

As expected, the U.S. got through group play undefeated. Then, in a replay of the 1995 World Cup, they found themselves in a semifinal face-off with Norway. Nearly 65,000 people packed into Stanford Stadium in Athens, Georgia, to see how the U.S. Olympic team would fare against the number one team in the world.

Unfortunately, right from the beginning it did not go well. The stunned pro-American crowd quieted as Norway's star, Linda Medalen, scored an early goal in the 10th minute. Would this game be a repeat of 1995? The Norwegians were famous for their rugged and stingy defense. One goal had been enough for them to beat the U.S. in the World Cup. Could it happen again?

The U.S. went into halftime, down 1-0. In the second half, the U.S. tried to find weaknesses in Norway's defense, but were denied again and again. The "Vikings" were not giving an inch. It was still 1-0 with just 20 minutes to play. It looked as if the game could end in another crushing defeat for the American team. But this time, it would be worse: it would happen in front of the largest home crowd to watch a women's soccer game in U.S. history.

Then they caught a break. Norwegian midfielder Agnete Carlsen was yellow carded for the second time in the game, and a red card followed. She was ejected and now the Norwegians had to continue the rest of the match a player short. It didn't take long for the Americans to take advantage of the situation. Five minutes later, Akers buried a penalty kick. The game was tied!

The match went into overtime. In the Olympics, the Golden Goal rule applied. Whoever scored first would win the game. The two squads, desperate for victory, battled back and forth, but Norway, still a player short, was tiring.

In the 100th minute, Julie Foudy ran with the ball and found an open Shannon MacMillian crossing toward the goal. Macmillan had been subbed in and was running on fresh legs. The pass from Foudy was perfect and MacMillan didn't hesitate to bury the ball in the goal to make it 2-1!

The United States had won!

The record crowd went wild as the Americans piled on top of each other in celebration. But even in their happiness, they had not forgiven nor forgotten the 1995 World Cup loss to Norway. Revenge was theirs.

"It was sweet to watch the Norwegians walk off the field," Michelle Akers said.

7

More than 76,000 spectators showed up at Stanford Stadium for the gold medal final against China on a hot Georgia night on August 1, 1996; the vast majority of them were cheering wildly for the Stars and Stripes. The support was overwhelming. "You'd lose your breath a little bit when you walked out there," Julie Foudy said.

The noisy crowd had reason to get even louder very early in the match. Shannon MacMillan, who tallied the dramatic, overtime, game-winning Golden Goal against Norway in the semifinal, put the U.S. on the board in the 19th minute. Kristine Lilly had crossed to Mia Hamm who blasted a shot at China's goalkeeper

Gao Hong. The goalie managed to parry the powerful effort off the right post, but it fell to an unmarked MacMillan who quickly dispatched it. Suddenly, the U.S. was leading 1-0 in the gold medal match.

China hadn't received the memo that they should roll over and let the Americans win. They responded by pushing numbers into the attack and trying to overrun the U.S. backline of Brandi Chastain, Carla Overbeck, and Joy Fawcett. The defense was struggling.

With the Americans back on their heels, Sun Wen, a forward who many compared to Mia Hamm and who would share the FIFA Women's Player of the Century award with Michelle Akers, deftly chipped the ball over American goalie Briana Scurry in the 32nd minute and scored.

The game was 1-1 going into halftime.

At the break, an exhausted and injured Hamm asked her teammates if she should come out. She didn't want to hurt the team's chances if she wasn't 100 percent. The response in the locker room was unanimous: No. They needed their best player on the field. It was obvious that Mia Hamm had become the new leader the team would rely on to carry them.

In the second half, the Americans weathered a Chinese surge and took back the momentum. Hamm, as if buoyed by her teammates' faith, nearly scored just 15 minutes into the second half. That shot on goal didn't succeed, but the Americans created another opportunity six minutes later. Once again, Hamm was involved. She diverted a pass to an overlapping Joy Fawcett who in turn directed a cross in front of the goal to Tiffeny Milbrett. The Chinese goalkeeper never had a chance. The University of Portland star buried the ball in the back of the net before the goalie could even react.

The Chinese could not recover and the U.S. won the first-ever women's soccer Olympic gold medal in front of a screaming and adoring home crowd.

Afterwards, Fawcett looked up into the stands and smiled while she held her two-year-old daughter, Katelyn, who had become something of a team mascot. Fawcett had rejoined the national squad just eight weeks after giving birth to her daughter. But she did so on one condition; she would come back if she could take her daughter with her to games and practices. Why should she choose between the game she loved and

having a family? Fawcett was determined she could
do both.

Katelyn became a fixture on the field and in the
training room, and she had some of the most talented
soccer players on the planet as babysitters. It wasn't
easy, but Fawcett overcame whatever obstacles were
in her path to make it happen. It seemed fitting that
Katelyn was there to share the team's gold medal
moment.

Also in the stands was Mia Hamm's older brother,
Garrett—her inspiration for playing soccer. There were
tears in his eyes as he hugged her on the field. She was
crying, too. He had made it to the Olympics despite
suffering from a rare blood disease. Mia was so happy
that he was there to watch their gold medal victory. It
would be the last time he would see her compete on the
world stage. Despite a valiant fight, he would die eight
months later.

On the victor's stand, the women's team was singing
again, but this time it wasn't Queen's "We Are The
Champions." It was the national anthem. Hands
on their hearts, their faces still gleaming with sweat
from the final match, the proud Americans watched

as the American flag was raised to the top position. They were number one in the world again. "We did it together. And here we were singing, badly," Foudy said. "Shouting the national anthem."

After winning the Olympic gold at home, the U.S. team felt that this had to be the moment when soccer finally arrived in the United States. This was the event that was going to change it all! But had it? NBC, the television network covering the 1996 Olympic Games, didn't even broadcast the game live in its entirety. NBC cut back to the game during its regular Olympic coverage. All-in-all, only about 30 minutes of the final match was televised. It seemed that NBC was much more interested in broadcasting another women's sport: gymnastics. While the network could find prime-time space to air features of American women gymnasts dancing to the Village People's "YMCA," it was having difficulty locating 76,000 screaming soccer fans cheering the women's soccer team on to a gold medal.

But while NBC paid the team minimum attention, something had changed. Word of mouth had generated a buzz about this group of elite women athletes who had brought home the gold. Advertisers that had shown no previous interest in Team U.S.A. suddenly noticed that Americans liked these women and wanted to know more about them.

Given her amazing skills, it was understandable that advertisers decided that Mia Hamm should be the face of U.S. Women's soccer. But it was ironic because of her selfless nature and quiet demeanor. It would be hard to find anyone else who shied more from the spotlight.

As Hamm became a familiar face to Americans through television commercials, products, and ads, people were becoming more and more aware that there was also an amazing women's soccer team behind her. In a sense, the U.S. team brought home gold in more ways than one at the 1996 Olympic Games, and the women's national team started to receive attention that was woefully past due.

8

The 1999 World Cup was scheduled to be played in the United States. At first, the World Cup organizing committee had planned to stage the event in small stadiums across the United States. But, once committee members saw the crowds of rabid fans that had come to large stadiums to watch the women compete in the 1996 Summer Games, they changed their minds. It was decided the matches would be held in large stadiums like Giants Stadium in New Jersey and the Rose Bowl in Pasadena, California.

The challenge was bringing the masses. The Rose Bowl alone could hold up to 100,000 fans and could look very empty if only a few thousand fans showed up.

It was ambitious and critics wondered out loud if large crowds would even come to women's soccer matches. One newspaper headline read, "What if they threw a World Cup and nobody came?"

The U.S. team went on the offensive to prove those critics wrong. Suddenly, the team was everywhere. It seemed there wasn't a youth soccer field they wouldn't visit or a clinic they wouldn't teach. In matches that led up to the World Cup, they would stay behind for hours signing autographs. Young girls with stars in their eyes would giggle and scream as they watched their heroes wow them with skills they hoped to master one day. The women of the national team were selling America on soccer and were selling tickets at the same time. Unlike an increasing number of elite male athletes who seemingly had forgotten their fans, the U.S. Women's National Soccer team embraced them and worked hard to win them over. "We wanted to be there for those kids," Mia Hamm said.

Despite confidently telling reporters at a press conference that "of course" the World Cup would sell out, co-team captain, Julie Foudy, was still nervous that people might not show up. "We better sell this out," she whispered to co-captain Carla Overbeck.

Months before the World Cup was to begin over 200,000 tickets had been sold. That was over 100,000 more tickets than had been sold at the entire 1995 World Cup in Sweden.

The matches leading up to the 1999 World Cup had been hard for Mia Hamm. She was devastated by the loss of her brother. The support of her teammates is what got her through the most difficult time of her life. They weren't just good teammates, they were also good friends. After taking a brief period of time off from the team, Mia came back and played like a woman possessed. In 1997, she scored 18 goals between May 2 and June 8 alone. She continued to work on her quickness and agility and had developed into the best player in the world. She was driven. It was as if she now played every game for the brother she had idolized and lost.

In 1998 the team played 25 matches and lost only one. The number one team in the world was playing like it. The squad was going into the 1999 World Cup in good form, but the pressure was still on. The American women were expected to win before the home crowd.

If they didn't play up to expectations, it would not only be embarrassing, but it could deal a devastating blow to women's soccer in the United States.

When the Americans took the field against Denmark to open the 1999 World Cup, they still weren't sure if people were going to show up. They didn't have to worry: a sold out crowd of 80,000 people crammed into Giants Stadium to cheer on the U.S. team. The players were astounded as their bus drove into the stadium parking lot and thousands of fans were tailgating and milling about. They had just stepped into the single largest women's-only sporting event in the history of the world.

When the team finally stepped on to the field, some were so emotional they started crying. "I think we all had goose bumps," Hamm said. "How could you not have goose bumps when you see the stadium filled and people chanting 'U-S-A, U-S-A'?" The overwhelming atmosphere concerned Coach DiCicco. Seeing his players overcome with emotion, he wondered if it would affect their play against Denmark. He needn't have been worried. The Americans blitzed through that game, winning easily 3-0. As expected, they got through group play fairly easily.

"We're not here to lose," Joy Fawcett told reporters.

But, they almost did exactly that against Germany in the quarterfinals.

In the game against Germany, the U.S. fell behind for the first time in the tournament on an errant back pass from Brandi Chastain to goalie Briana Scurry that found its way into the U.S. goal. An own goal! The U.S. went into half-time down 2-1. At the half-time break co-captain Carla Overbeck told the team, "Everything we've done in this lifetime comes down to these next 45 minutes. We have 45 minutes to make a difference. That's it. We have to leave everything on the field."

In the second half, Chastain found redemption when she evened the score on a beautiful goal. Joy Fawcett then put the U.S. ahead for good on a header from a corner kick. The Americans had escaped Jack Kent Cooke Stadium in Maryland with a 3-2 victory. After a relatively easy semifinal 2-0 win over Brazil in front of 73,000 fans in Palo Alto, California, the home side reached the final against a Chinese squad that had beaten them in 2 out of 3 earlier friendly matches.

The country talked nonstop about the highly

anticipated final that would be played in the Rose Bowl in Pasadena, California. Even President Bill Clinton planned to attend, saying, "The whole country is caught up. It's going to have a bigger impact than people ever realized, and it will have a far-reaching impact not only in the United States but also in other countries."

On July 10, 1999, a record-breaking 90,000 people were in attendance to watch the final; a rematch of the 1996 Olympic gold medal game. The U.S. knew that if it was going to win, it needed to stop Chinese forward, Sun Wen, a remarkable striker who would eventually be named the best player in the tournament. They turned to Michelle Akers to defend this dangerous player.

Despite her Chronic Fatigue Syndrome, Akers gave everything she had. With a minute left in regulation play, she collapsed. Despite being physically exhausted, she wanted to stay in the game. The team doctor finally said no, and the American star was ushered into the locker room. The hard-fought battle was even at 0-0 at the end of regulation play and went into overtime.

The Chinese immediately attacked the area where Michelle Akers had been. If not for the heroics of Kristine Lilly who was standing on the goal line when she headed away a well-placed header by the Chinese in overtime, the match would have been lost and it wouldn't have gone to penalty kicks.

The huge crowd quieted as the Chinese and the Americans swapped penalty kick scores. On the third kick by the Chinese, goalkeeper Briana Scurry came up big and swatted away Liu Ying's attempt. On the fourth kick Hamm for the U.S. and Zang Ouying for China evenly scored. And then the Chinese scored with their fifth attempt—their fourth goal in the penalty shootout. The score sheet was 4-4, but the U.S. still had to make their last attempt to win it all.

The potential match-winning kick was up to a player who just three years earlier had not even been certain she would ever be on the U.S. squad again, much less standing before a crowd of 90,000 people and some 40 million television viewers with the World Cup championship on the line.

Brandi Chastain was at the mark. Alone.

The young Californian stood over the ball, her long blonde hair held back in a ponytail.

She looked at the ball, but never looked at the Chinese goalie. She had missed a penalty kick in a previous match against the Chinese. Moments before, Chastain had been lying face down on the ground, wondering if her calves were going to cramp. Now that didn't matter. She took four quick steps, then blasted the ball towards the goal with her powerful left foot. The shot was true as it headed for the net to Gao's left. "It was like everything happened really quickly, but it was in slow motion," Chastain said.

Gao anticipated correctly and dove to her left, but the rocket off of Chastain's left foot was too powerful for the Chinese goalie to stop. The ball hit the back of the net and almost instantly, Chastain ripped off her jersey, sank to her knees, and pumped her fists. "It was momentary insanity, nothing more, nothing less," she said. That image would appear on the cover of *Sports Illustrated* the next week and would become the photograph millions of fans remembered when they thought of the 1999 World Cup.

Chastain's teammates mobbed the defender as 90,000 fans exploded into deafening cheers.

But Chastain hadn't been the only person to lose her jersey during the game. Akers, who had been helped off the field, was so weak that doctors had to cut off her jersey in the locker room to give her some IVs and hook her up to an EKG machine. She had been watching the remainder of game from the locker room, barely able to move, when Chastain made her historic shot. The fierce competitor ripped out the IVs so she could go onto the field to celebrate. There was no stopping her from being with her teammates in this amazing moment.

They had done it. They were World Cup champions, again.

If people in the United States hadn't been aware of the women's national team before, they knew about them now. Women's soccer had finally broken through the ceiling and was on the map in a big way. It was not only a victory for women's soccer, but it was a victory for women's athletics. "We did it. We made it. We're here," Mia Hamm said.

9

n February of 2000, following the wild success of
the 1999 World Cup, the Women's United Soccer
Association (WUSA) was formed. For the first
time, women soccer players in the United States had
a professional league of their own. What was once
considered a hobby had been now been given the status
of a profession, with the top players bringing in over
$100,000 a year. It was not nearly what the top-tier
men were making around the world, but it was a start.

The formation of the new league promoted the
development of future stars. One of those stars, Abby
Wambach, got her start playing alongside Mia Hamm
for the Washington Freedom. While some women

were enjoying the experience of their new league, the women's national team had another challenge to meet that year: the 2000 Olympic Games in Sydney, Australia.

April Heinrichs had been named the squad's new head coach. It was a historic move, as Heinrichs was not only an ex-player for the national team, but she was the first woman coach given the nod for the position. Could she bring the same success that the male coaches, Dorrance and DiCicco, had brought to the national team? All eyes were on her. If Heinrichs was to continue the team's winning ways, she would have to do it without the legendary Michelle Akers. Just three weeks before the Olympics, she announced her retirement. Injury and disease had finally taken its toll on the American team's first superstar. Akers left the team with a remarkable legacy: 136 goals in international competition. Only four people, men or women, had scored more than 100 goals in international play. "I have huge peace knowing that I fought to the very end and have nothing left to give," she said upon retirement.

As expected, the U.S. team had a fairly easy run on its

way to the gold medal round in Australia, where they were to play against the nemesis that just wouldn't go away.

They were once again face-to-face with the hated "Vikings." While the United States was considered the best team in the world, Norway was not intimidated. At first, it looked as if the Americans would make easy work of it. The Stars and Stripes scored in the first five minutes. Hamm, of course, did the work. She beat Goeril Kringen, pushing past the helpless Norwegian defender with ease, then crossing back to Tiffeny Milbrett whose chip found the back of the net.

Even the tough Norwegians had their doubts after that goal. "When the U.S. team scored very early I thought 'No, not again. Why should they win again and again and again?'" Norway's Gro Espeseth said.

The Americans had the match under control until the end of the first half, when Hege Riise sent in a corner kick that Espeseth met with her head. The score was tied 1-1 at halftime.

In the second half, Norway's Ragnhild Gulbrandsen made it 2-1 Norway in the 78th minute. Suddenly, the invincible United States was looking very vulnerable.

With only 30 seconds to go in regulation play, it was looking bleak for the Americans. Hamm, once again, came to the rescue. She burst down the right side and launched a curling cross into the box. Milbrett, who always seemed to know exactly where Hamm was trying to place the ball, leapt into the air and redirected it into the back of the net. Tie game.

Overtime. Yet again.

It wouldn't last that long. Instead of folding after conceding the last-second strike, Norway refocused and went on the attack. A long ball to Norwegian Dagny Mellgren fell between two American defenders who were marking her. In what looked to be a clear handball by Mellgren, the ball was redirected in front of her, where she had a clear, uncontested path to goal. No hand ball was called and she buried the goal to make it a Norwegian win, leaving the exhausted and tearful U.S. holding the silver medal. At least the Norwegians did not repeat their performance of "The Train" after this game, but it was little consolation.

After the match, Julie Foudy went up to the referee and said to her, "You are going to see this video and you are going to want this back. You just crushed every dream that I had. So sleep well tonight." Still, the Norwegians had their revenge.

The Americans were not going home with the gold. In the locker room after the heartbreaking game, Hamm addressed her teammates. "Hold your head high and be proud," she said through tears. The squad was defeated but not beaten. They would be back.

10

After their Olympic loss, captain Carla Overbeck retired from the team, leaving the core of Chastain, Foudy, Fawcett, Lilly, and Hamm as the veterans of the squad. The "kids" were all grown up now and were considered the old-timers. They were nicknamed "the 91ers" because they were all that was left of the 1991 World Championship team.

But there was a new kid on the block. In 2001 a tall, strong striker joined the team. Her name was Abby Wambach. Like Akers, she had competed on boys' teams growing up, and, like Akers, she was tough as nails. She grew up idolizing Hamm and even had an autographed poster of her. Wambach brought to the

U.S. team the skill set of Hamm combined with the physicality of Akers. If someone were to build a perfect striker, she would look a lot like Abby Wambach.

As the 2003 World Cup approached, some were questioning whether the U.S. was fielding its best team for the international tournament. While the U.S. team had added some fresh, new talent in Abby Wambach in 2001 and Shannon Boxx in 2003, there were some doubts whether the older players were up to the task.

Amid that controversy, women's soccer was dealt a huge blow. Just a few days before the World Cup, the WUSA folded. Lack of ticket sales and corporate sponsorship was blamed. The women's professional league in the United States was officially dead after only three years of existence. A mixture of doubt, loss, sadness, and expectation followed the team into the 2003 World Cup.

The tournament, originally scheduled to be held in China, was moved to the United States at the last minute because of the SARS epidemic in China. It represented a chance for the Americans to defend their title on home soil again. The U.S. women were ecstatic to play in front of home crowds.

In group play the Red, White, and Blue won all three matches by a combined score of 11-1. The squad seemed to be proving the critics wrong again. Hamm, Foudy, and Lilly tallied for the 91ers, while Wambach and Boxx also proved their prowess. Wambach netted the game-winner in a tense 1-0 victory over archrival Norway in the quarterfinal at Gillette Stadium in Foxboro, Massachusetts.

The U.S. was set to play the Germans in the semifinals. In their quarterfinal match, Germany had dismantled Russia 7-1. It looked like the Germans were for real and that the United States would have a hard-fought battle on their hands. On October 5, 2003, Germany, led by Birgit Prinz, sent the U.S. home after a 3-0 victory. The Americans beat Canada for the third-place medal, but it was Germany that raised the trophy on October 12 at The Home Depot Center in Carson, California.

After the 2003 World Cup, it was clear that the 91ers were nearing the end of their careers. They would all play together for the last time in the 2004 Olympics in Athens, Greece and they were determined to go out with a bang.

And they did. Fittingly, Wambach—the future of women's soccer—led the squad in scoring with four goals, including yet another powerful header in overtime to win the gold-medal game against Brazil. Hamm had two during the competition and Lilly netted three while also earning the assist on Wambach's gold-medal winning score.

"It's a fabulous way to win an Olympic gold medal, and it's an even better way to send off these women, because they're what this is about," Wambach said of the 2-1 victory over Brazil. "This is not about me or the younger players. It's about them."

Although Lilly would continue playing for the team along with Brandi Chastain, the 91ers had won their final medal together. In the post-game celebration, there were smiles, not tears. They had accomplished great things and had helped put women's soccer on the map in the United States and internationally.

After the Olympics, the squad went on a ten-game farewell tour, going 9-0-1 between September and December of 2004. In the final match, which ended in a 5-0 victory over Mexico, Wambach, the new U.S. superstar, scored two goals. It was clear that the baton had been passed to the next generation.

After the match against Mexico at the Home Depot Center in Carson, California, was over, the real celebration began. None of the 15,000-plus supporters left the stadium. They wanted to see Hamm, Foudy, and Fawcett. As the three women—with nearly 800 international appearances between them—raised their arms to salute the adoring fans for one last time, a seemingly endless wave of applause crashed over them.

They had earned this praise with their impressive play, tireless promotion of the game, and dedication to winning and playing the right way. They had been through thick and thin together, this first generation of female American soccer stars.

Mia Hamm had played in 275 games and had scored 158 international goals, a record that would stand for many years until Wambach eventually broke it. During her playing career, she had created countless memories and millions of fans. Julie Foudy had 271 caps over her 17-year career, and Joy Fawcett, the stalwart defender had donned the American uniform 239 times. Together they had helped forge a women's national team from an entity that had had been literally ignored into an internationally renowned and respected program. It seemed like a million years ago that they had been the "kids," but they knew it was time for a new generation of American stars to take the field. They were certain they were leaving the team they had loved and nurtured in good hands, as they waved one last farewell as the Los Angeles sun set in the distance.

11

Greg Ryan, April Heinrich's assistant, took over the American squad in 2005, understanding he had a team in transition. He had a mix of young and veteran players and had inherited talented attackers in Wambach and Boxx, as well as a young goalkeeper named Hope Solo. He needed a goalkeeper to eventually replace Briana Scurry, the veteran goalkeeper who had been a fixture in the American net since 1994. Solo, a veteran of the U.S. youth program, was the obvious choice. At five feet, nine inches tall, she was bigger than most female goalies, but displayed the type of quickness one would expect from someone who was much smaller. Solo had been an all-American forward and record-setting goal scorer in high school. She moved to goal when she attended the University of Washington, although she admitted that she didn't love goalkeeping until pretty late in her college career. She won the Hermann award for the best college soccer player in the nation her senior year.

But she could be as trying as she was talented. Solo was the product of a difficult upbringing in the Pacific Northwest. She was outspoken and had a strong personality that rubbed some people the wrong way. She didn't always get along with her teammates, but they always appreciated her talents. Under Ryan, Solo started seeing much more playing time and responded well to it. She didn't concede a single goal in the seven starts she tallied in 2005.

In 2006 Solo earned the majority of the playing time—posting shutouts over countries like China, Japan, and Australia—while veteran Briana Scurry primarily played a backup role.

The world had been put on notice: not only did the U.S. have an impressive attack led by the ever-improving Wambach, the unceasing brilliance of Kristine Lilly, and the exploits of young Ali Wagner and Heather O'Reilly, but they also had to beat the best keeper in the world. That is, if they ever managed to get a shot past the rock-solid backline.

The U.S. didn't lose a match in 2005 or 2006. Anyone who was paying attention was not surprised. This was a very good U.S. team.

Just before the United States team faced off with North Korea in its first group game in the 2007 World Cup held in China, Ryan made a bold statement that surely didn't sit well with the Brazilians or the defending World Cup champions, Germany. "I think we're the favorites," he said. "So far we've outplayed every international team we've faced, and that includes pretty much all the top teams other than Brazil."

The Americans didn't look like the favorites in their first game, however, as they fought to a 2-2 draw against the North Koreans. But the team got back on track after impressive wins over organized Sweden and athletic Nigeria. The U.S. then easily dispatched England in the quarterfinal.

Hope Solo had started in net for the U.S. the entire World Cup. But when the team came out on the field for the semifinal game against the Brazilians, it was

Briana Scurry who was taking warm-up shots in goal. What the 50,000 spectators at the Yellow Dragon Stadium in Hangzhou didn't know was that Ryan had told the team in a meeting before the game that the veteran Scurry was going to start in goal against the dangerous Brazilians rather than Solo. His reasoning was that 36-year-old Scurry, who had over 150 international starts to her name, had played in more big games. And the match against Brazil was a huge game. Facing the most dangerous player in the world in Brazil's astounding Marta and her equally cunning teammate, Cristiane, he felt that experience trumped youth and athleticism for this match. Scurry was going to get the start.

Not surprisingly, Hope Solo was furious. She felt it was personal. Her father had died several weeks before the start of the Cup and she had dedicated this World Cup to him. She had started the last nine matches for the United States. It didn't seem right and it didn't seem fair. As the television cameras zoomed in on Solo sitting on the bench, she made no attempt to hide her anger.

Almost immediately, it was clear Ryan made the

wrong choice. Scurry appeared slow and overwhelmed. For that matter, so did the rest of the U.S. squad. The first Brazilian goal came on a corner kick. Formiga curled the kick to the near post and Leslie Osborne dove to head the ball out of bounds. Instead, the midfielder accidentally deflected it into the net. Scurry, who didn't call Osborne off the ball, was helpless to do anything.

Scurry may not have been entirely to blame for the first goal, but she could have done better on the next one, which came just seven minutes later. Marta cut in from the right side and took a soft shot with her excellent left foot. Scurry dove to her left, but failed to reach the ball as it rolled into the net. Solo, watching, felt it was a shot she could have saved if she were in goal. Things just got worse for the U.S. when Shannon Boxx, the team's best midfielder, was sent off just before halftime.

It was a dismal showing and by the time it was over, Cristiane had a goal, Marta had two, and the Brazilians had destroyed the Americans 4-0.

Post-match, Solo ripped into Ryan's decision to start Scurry in goal. As usual, she spoke with her heart first.

"It was the wrong decision, and I think anybody who knows anything about the game knows that," she said. "There's no doubt in my mind I would have made those saves... You can't live by big names. You can't live in the past."

Her words were strong and honest, and immediately created a rift on the team. She had stepped over an invisible line and broken the code that you don't bad-talk coaches or other players in front of the press. "These codes aren't in writing," Ryan said. "It's not a legal code; it's a personal code, a code of a community of players who care about one another and work for one another."

Some veterans of the squad met with Solo and demanded an apology. The angry women felt that Solo had thrown another team member under the bus and that was inexcusable. Some even said it was "treason." In a meeting with the whole team the next morning, it was decided—Solo was out. Ryan suspended her from the team. She couldn't suit up for the consolation match against Norway, she couldn't stay with the team, and she couldn't fly back home with the team. She had been effectively banished and would never be a member of the U.S. national team as long as Ryan was coach.

Which wouldn't be for long. Despite his impressive winning record of 45-1-9 over three years with the national team, Ryan was fired by the U.S. Soccer Federation in October. They cited his failures in the World Cup as well as his controversial decision to start Scurry against Brazil as the reasons for letting him go.

So now the U.S. team was divided and in disarray and in need of a new coach. With the 2008 Beijing Olympics only a year away, healing was going to have to begin, and it was going to have to begin quickly if the U.S. was going to have a chance to win gold.

12

nto the fray stepped new coach, Pia Sundhage, a former Swedish national player who had finished sixth in the 2000 voting for FIFA Women's Player of the Century. She had served as an assistant with China in 2007 and knew some of the American players, including the captain, Kristine Lilly, from her stint as head coach at KIF Örebro DFF. In her very first meeting with the U.S. national team, she broke out an acoustic guitar and started singing Bob Dylan's "The Times They Are a Changin'."

"It was a fifty-fifty chance they would say this is a crazy coach or this is a coach we want to follow," Sundhage said. "I had to be myself." After she finished the song, she looked up and Abby Wambach and several other players started clapping. "We went from there," Sundhage said.

Sundhage was perhaps the perfect coach to step into the divided American locker room. She described her attitude in life and coaching as "a glass half full" and if there was a problem she would put on her "possible glasses" to see what she could do to make things work. The first thing she needed to put on her 'possible glasses' for was the situation with Hope Solo. Some of Solo's teammates, especially some of the veterans from the 1999 World Cup team, were so angry at her that they refused to even talk to her, let alone consider her reinstatement to the team.

Sundhage sat the squad down and asked them two simple questions: "Do you want to win?" and "Do you need goalkeepers to win?" The answer to both, obviously, was a resounding "yes," even from the women who felt most aggrieved by Solo's actions.

Sundhage knew that Hope Solo was one of the best goalkeepers in the world and was asking her team to put the past behind them and look forward to what would be best for the national team. She decided that Solo needed to be on the team and reinstated her.

Solo's climb back didn't happen overnight, but slowly she began to work herself back into the good graces of her teammates. She issued an apology through U.S. Soccer in October of 2007. It was a start. She knew that in some cases, she would never be accepted back into the fold on a personal level, especially by some of the veterans.

Always blunt, Solo stated, "We don't have to be friends to respect what somebody does on the field."

Sundhage had confidence in her, starting her in 27 games in 2008. She recorded 13 shutouts in those matches. Leading up to the 2008 Olympic Games in Beijing, Solo was starting to feel comfortable on the squad again. "Time has really been the great healer. I know a lot of us have done some deep soul-searching," she said. "I'm genuinely enjoying my teammates again, which I never thought was possible."

Sundhage's "possible glasses" had worked. The U.S. team appeared strong and cohesive leading to the Olympic Games.

Then disaster struck.

Cat Whitehill, one of the team's best defenders,

injured her left knee in a June warmup. Another unthinkable event happened a month later. In a July exhibition against Brazil, Abby Wambach crashed into defender Andreia Rosa and fell to the ground, her leg broken. The American gold medal hopes, which rested so heavily on Wambach's powerful shoulders, looked broken as well.

Going into the Olympic Games, the Americans had been the favorites. That was no longer the case. The U.S. lost 2-0 to Norway in the opening match. The team looked lost. They were unsure of how to score without Wambach or how to defend without Whitehill.

But they had Sundhage's sunny perspective and the discipline she brought to the team. They didn't panic. Carli Lloyd netted an impressive and important goal in the next match, a 1-0 victory over Japan. A 4-0 win against New Zealand put the Stars and Stripes into the quarterfinal where they were set to meet Canada. The U.S. defeated Canada and then Japan in the semifinals. Once again, the U.S. found itself in the gold-medal match, facing the same Brazilian team that had humiliated them in the semifinal match in the World Cup less than a year earlier.

Unlike the 2007 World Cup match, Hope Solo would be in goal. There would be no controversy this time. Just eleven months before, few would have predicted that the U.S.—led by Solo—would be battling for gold. But nobody thought the U.S. stood a chance against the powerful and talented Brazilians.

From the first whistle, Brazil was the aggressor. Marta, two-time FIFA Player of the Year, was everywhere. Cristiane's skill and athleticism proved nearly impossible to contain. It was no surprise that she led the tournament in goals scored. And yet, the South Americans could not get on the board. Time and time again, Solo was a wall they kept running into.

Ninety minutes came and went. The referee had added stoppage time to the match. The Brazilians redoubled their efforts, but still couldn't score. In the 96th minute, however, it was the U.S. that would find the back of the net. Forward Amy Rodriguez managed to hold off two defenders long enough to pass to Carli Lloyd, who took a touch, then ripped a left-footed shot from just outside the 18-yard box.

Impossibly, the U.S. had taken the lead. The desperate Brazilians took several shots on goal, but once again were frustrated by Solo. When the final whistle blew, the Brazilians, and many of the 51,610 spectators in the stands, stood stunned as they watched the Americans celebrate their second consecutive Olympic gold medal.

Once again, the U.S. sang the national anthem on the victor's stand... this time, without a guitar accompaniment from Sundhage.

13

The United States almost didn't qualify to play in the 2011 World Cup in Germany. The American team started focusing on the upcoming World Cup almost immediately after winning the gold medal in Beijing. They returned home for a victory tour, going 7-0-1, then prepared to go through the CONCACAF World Cup qualification. In the past, this had been a mere formality. The U.S. usually breezed through qualification. By the time the U.S. squad met the Mexican team in the CONCACAF semifinal game, the Americans had outscored their opponents 18-0. It looked like another easy World Cup qualification for the women's team. Mexico had not beaten the U.S. in

25 previous attempts.

But the beautiful game can also be a cruel one.

Despite a 17-8 advantage in shots by the Americans, the Mexican home crowd of 8,500 at Estadio Beto Avila witnessed the impossible. Mexico beat the Americans 2-1. The stunned U.S. squad was on the verge of being disqualified! Was it possible that one of the best teams in the world wouldn't be playing in soccer's biggest event?

Luckily, the U.S. team still had hope. After beating Costa Rica in the third-place match, they needed to defeat Italy during a two-game series. Only then could they make up for their losses and qualify. And once again, it was time for new batch of up-and-coming American stars to shine.

In the first match, they defeated the Italians on their home soil in Padova. A young striker named Alex Morgan came in as a substitute in the second half to score the winning goal. A week later in Bridgeview, Illinois, Amy Rodriguez scored the winning goal, and the Americans walked away with a second 1-0 victory. They were going to Germany after all!

But they would be going to the World Cup without another of the original 91ers. In January of 2011, Kristine Lilly announced her retirement. Over the course of more than two decades, Lilly won an astounding 352 caps. She had played in five World Cups and three Olympics and had competed against 39 different countries, scoring against 30 of them. "When I sit here and realize that it's been 23 or 24 years since I started playing at this level, when I think about those numbers it does seem like a really long journey," Lilly said during an emotional goodbye. "But the best thing is that I've had the opportunity in the last five or ten years to really appreciate the impact we've made, not only on the field, but off the field with young people as well and I'm really happy I was able to be a part of this for so long." There was little doubt it was the end of an era with the retirement of this well-respected American legend.

While they were still a very good team, the Americans had been struggling with consistency. Their loss to Mexico in the CONCACAF semifinals was testament to that. But they were also a team that found ways to win in very tough matches.

Once again, their consistency was questioned when they finished second to the Swedes in group play at the 2011 World Cup. If the U.S. was going to continue to make it through the knockout rounds, they would have to scrape and claw their way down that path. Unfortunately, once again, the tough and talented Brazilians were standing in that path in the quarterfinals.

As expected, that game against the Brazilians, played in Dresden, Germany, was tight and hard fought. After a 1-1 draw, the match went into over-time. Then the unstoppable Marta scored for the Brazilians in the 92nd minute. One hundred minutes came and went. Then 110 minutes. Finally, the clock struck 120 minutes. The U.S. was down a goal with only seconds remaining. They were desperate and it looked like they would need a miracle to stay in the World Cup. They found one in the miraculous head of Abby Wambach.

With the ball at her feet at the 122nd minute in extended time, Megan Rapinoe looked up and saw her friend and teammate, Wambach, in the goal box. Rapinoe, with her short, dyed-blonde hair atop her five-foot, seven-inch frame, blasted a curling, left-footed cross toward the striker. It was a perfect pass. Using her strength and instincts, Wambach rose above a Brazilian defender and a leaping goalie and sent a powerful header into the back of the net. The game was tied!

The stunned Brazilians could only wonder what had just happened as time ran out just a little more than a minute later. They had lost the 2008 Olympic gold medal to the U.S. on a Wambach header, and now that same head had stolen their sure berth into the semifinals of the World Cup. It was the header heard around the world.

Now this 2011 World Cup match was going to be decided on penalty kicks. It was a daunting task for the Brazilians who now had to face Hope Solo one-on-one. This time, it was Solo's turn to shine. Wambach and Solo didn't exactly see eye-to-eye on things, but the veteran Wambach knew their goalkeeper would come through. "She has the confidence you always want to see," Wambach said.

In the shootout, she exhibited that confidence and more. Cristiane and Marta scored, as did Shannon Boxx and Carli Lloyd for the Americans. Daiane, the Brazilian center defender, stepped to the spot. She took her run up to the ball and kicked. Solo guessed right, diving to her right. She managed to get her right hand on the ball and swatted it away from the goal. It was a critical and amazing save.

Wambach and Rapinoe made their kicks in short order, as did a Brazilian. With the game at 4-3, Ali Krieger stepped to the mark to take the potential game-winning kick.

It seemed fitting that Krieger would be on the spot for that kick. She was lucky to be on any field at all. While playing for Penn State in 2005, she had almost died from blood clots in her lungs. Doctors said she had experienced six mini-heart attacks and was lucky to be alive. That she was still breathing at all was testament to her strong heart and will. Krieger proved that her heart still beat strong as she sunk the match-winning goal. The Americans had somehow done it! They were moving on.

Pandemonium raged on the field as the Americans celebrated. Millions watching on television had just witnessed one of the most exciting and heart stopping games in women's World Cup history, courtesy of a last-minute header by Wambach.

Pia Sundage later said it was her favorite memory of her time with the U.S. team.

The Americans won a tough match against the French in the semifinals and found themselves in the finals, ready to face Japan, a disciplined team that had been playing the best soccer of the tournament. The U.S. squad was confident they would give Japan a run for its money. They were beginning to sense that they were a team of destiny and that they would finally be bringing the Cup back to the United States after an absence of 12 long years.

"This is our journey, this is our dream," Wambach said. "I have belief in this team. Everybody is working for each other."

Could this be the year?

14

While the Americans were feeling like it was their destiny to win, there was another squad feeling the same at the 2011 World Cup. Although the Japanese hadn't beaten the U.S. squad in 25 previous attempts, this team was different. They were not only fast and technical, but they were playing with a mission. Earlier in the year, Japan had been hit by a devastating 9.0 earthquake, followed by an unimaginably destructive tsunami. It was an unprecedented natural disaster that resulted in a nuclear plant meltdown, the destruction of thousands of buildings, and the deaths of more than 15,000 people. The Japanese team felt that their nation needed them to win to help them take their minds off of the horrible events at home. The Japanese were not only playing for the World Cup trophy, but for the entire country of Japan. The hardships they had endured went beyond soccer and into the very soul of their people. There was little doubt the Japanese were the sentimental favorites of the tournament.

But there couldn't be two teams of destiny. One team would go home with the trophy and another would not.

Before the final match began, nearly 50,000 spectators in Frankfurt and millions more set to watch the final on television witnessed the Japanese team holding up signs thanking "our friends around the world" who had responded to the devastating earthquake and tsunami with aid and support. Despite this emotional charge going into the game, it looked like the U.S. was the team to beat in the final. Observers thought the Americans, with their strength and athleticism, were more deeply talented than a Japanese team known for its precision passing and control of possession.

The Americans struck first when Team U.S.A.'s speedy young star, Alex Morgan, scored in the 69th minute. It seemed that the team of destiny was indeed the United States. The Japanese put the U.S. on notice that the Americans weren't the only ones who could engage in last-minute heroics. Aya Miyama found the net in the 81st minute after a mistake from Ali Krieger to send the match into overtime. Once again, Wambach's head starred in overtime. Twenty-two-year old Morgan, the youngest player on the squad, put a lovely cross to Wambach and reliable Wambach didn't miss the header. The U.S. found itself ahead, 2-1, with just sixteen minutes remaining.

As the U.S. squad had proven in its miraculous victory over Brazil, the game isn't over until it is over. With just three minutes left in overtime, Japan's team captain and veteran star player, Homara Sawa scored off a corner kick that sent the match into familiar territory for Team U.S.A.: penalty kicks.

So two teams of destiny faced off. The Americans were exhausted from a difficult tournament that had featured some legendary comebacks. The Japanese had staged two amazing comebacks in this match alone just to get to this point. Whose year was it going to be?

Japanese goalie, Ayumi Kaihori, saved Shannon

Boxx's attempt, then Lloyd missed, Tobin Heath had her shot saved, and Wambach scored. Solo managed to keep Yuki Nagasato's shot out of the net, but Miyama and Mizuho Sakaguchi both scored.

Saki Kumagai was at the mark and had to either miss her attempt or Solo would have to save the shot for the Americans to have a chance. Kumagai didn't blink. She calmly slotted her effort past Solo, then exploded into celebration with her teammates.

Despite all of the comebacks and the last-minute heroics, the Americans had not been the team of destiny. That honor had gone to Japan in 2011.

The valiant American contingent could only look on, destroyed but strangely okay. They had given their all and had come up short, but if they had to lose, then there was no shame in losing to the resilient Japanese squad.

"As much as I wanted this, if there's any team I could have given this to it's Japan," Solo said in a television interview as she held back tears. "So I'm happy for them."

Midfielder Lauren Cheney summed the conflicting emotions up best. "It wasn't a great feeling watching it slip away. Our team fought so much. I'm so proud of them. We've beaten so many odds. I love this team so much."

Despite the disappointment, the U.S. team was going to have to put the 2011 World Cup behind it and look forward to the 2012 Olympic Games in London.

15

After the 2011 World Cup, it was clear that the U.S. had another rising star in its midst.

Although Alex Morgan hadn't started in any of the games the U.S. had played at the 2011 World Cup, she had been a sub in five of the six games played. She had certainly made herself known. She scored a goal against France in the semifinal game and, in the match against Japan, she was the first player in women's World Cup history to record both a goal and an assist in a final.

Although it had appeared that Morgan had come out of nowhere, coach Pia Sundhage had been bringing her along, little by little. Even after Morgan's impressive

World Cup debut, Sundhage said that Morgan had to be patient and try not to move ahead too quickly in her career. "If she works on her technique... and adds that with reading the game, she could be very, very good— one of the best players in this country," Sunhdage said. "But the key again is for her to remember where she comes from, not to be too eager to get to the next step."

There was fire and determination in the youngster that Sundhage could appreciate. In an Olympic qualifying game against Mexico, the coach benched the rising star. Afterward, Sundhage asked her how she felt about it and Morgan replied, "To be honest, you really don't want to know how I'm feeling."

Morgan started in the next game against Canada and remained in the starting lineup from then on. The more Morgan played the more she and Wambach developed an unspoken understanding of each other on the field. They played to each other's strengths. Morgan had speed and creativity, while Wambach was brilliant in the air and could strike from distance. This combination of speed and strength, experience and youth, proved to be unstoppable up front.

Their formidable teamwork was never clearer than

in the Americans' first three matches of 2012. The duo combined for nine goals and two assists in dominating victories over China, Sweden, and Japan. The game against Japan was the most impressive, with the U.S. obliterating the 2011 World Cup winners 4-1 at a tournament in Sweden. Morgan and Wambach set the tone early with goals in the third minute and tenth minute, respectively. But dominating in Sweden and dominating at the Olympics were two different tasks. The best of the best qualified for London, and the U.S. found itself on the group stage with the always excellent France, rapidly improving Colombia, and unknown North Korea.

The U.S. survived the first game against France after it was down 2-0 in the first 14 minutes before a stunned 18,090 fans at Glasgow's Hampden Park. But the U.S. didn't panic, chipping away at the lead, getting two goals from Morgan and one each from Wambach and Carli Lloyd for a 4-2 victory.

Relatively easy wins over Colombia and North Korea in the group stage followed, as did a 2-0 victory against New Zealand. After a goal against the Kiwis, the women performed cartwheels in honor of American gymnast Gabby Douglas.

The semifinal game against the Canadians at Manchester's famous Old Trafford was a trench war. The Canadian's star, Christine Sinclair, was unstoppable. On three separate occasions she put the Maple Leafs on top. On the U.S. side, Rapinoe answered with two goals and Wambach with one. With the score 3-3 knotted at the end of regulation, the game went into overtime. Nearing the end of overtime, it looked like the game was going to penalty kicks, but with less than half a minute remaining, Alex Morgan outjumped defender Chelsea Stewart to meet a cross from Heather O'Reilly. Morgan, who was not known for the strength of her air game, headed the ball, and it floated tantalizingly over the Canadian goalie and into the back of the net. The U.S. was going to the gold medal game where they would face Japan in a rematch of the 2011 World Cup.

"It's everything. It's why we're here," Wambach said in a post-game interview. "This is what we are. This is who we are. This is what we've been working for."

London's Wembley Stadium crammed 80,203 people into its seats to witness history. The defending

World Cup champions, Japan, were playing against the defending Gold Medal champions, the U.S.A. While the Japanese owned the World Cup, the Americans felt like they owned the gold and the Japanese would have a fight on their hands to take it.

It didn't take long for the U.S. to claim ownership. Morgan took a pass from another rising star, Tobin Heath, and deftly chipped the ball into the box in the eighth minute. While Wambach could have taken it, the forward conceded the ball to her teammate, Lloyd, who was charging in on the ball, preparing to head it in. "I'll take Carli Lloyd's head any day over my foot," Wambach said. Lloyd, who had only made the Olympic roster as a replacement for an injured player, made the most of the opportunity. Goalkeeper Miho Fukumoto had no chance. The score was 1-0 U.S.

The U.S. knew that Japan was no pushover, and they were right. The Japanese pushed forward, forcing multiple saves from Hope Solo and a goal-line clearance from team captain Christie Rampone. After 45 minutes, the score stood, but in the second half Lloyd struck again. Taking the ball at midfield, she dribbled just outside the middle of the 18-yard box. There were a couple of U.S. players open on the wings. The Japanese sensed this and gave Lloyd a little room, expecting her to pass it off. But, unexpectedly, Lloyd kept charging ahead and released a hard right-foot shot that found its way in on the left side of the goal. It would not be the last time Lloyd surprised the Japanese with an unexpected shot on goal.

Her teammates mobbed her, while Lloyd yelled over the noise of 80,000 screaming fans, "We're not letting them back into the game."

On the other end of the field, American goalkeeper, Hope Solo, pumped her fists. The goal had come in the 54th minute and it put the Stars and Stripes up 2-0. Although Japan's Yuki Ogimi would score nine minutes later, the U.S. team would not concede another goal.

The Americans had their second straight gold medal and some revenge for the loss in 2011. The team celebrated on the field in London—Rapinoe crying tears of joy, Rampone jumping into Wambach's arms, and Solo dancing on her own. Afterwards, the team put on t-shirts that said, "Greatness Has Been Found." Lloyd found her own personal redemption, showing her coach that she had always belonged on the best team in the world.

"She proved that I was wrong and that I'm not that perfect," Sundhage said with typical honesty.

Team U.S.A. returned to the States as conquering heroes. Soon, however, they would be without a coach as Sundhage decided she wanted to return to her native Sweden to coach the Swedish national team.

It was somehow fitting that Pia Sundhage's last match as head of the United States Women's National Team should end in song. Except this time, it was the team singing to her, not the other way around. Abby Wambach, Megan Rapinoe, Alex Morgan, and the rest of the team serenaded their departing coach with "You Are My Sunshine" under a clear night sky. It was a fitting end to a near-perfect tenure.

The U.S. women's squad had just defeated Australia 6-2 in front of nearly 19,000 fans at Dick's Sporting Goods Park in Commerce City, Colorado. The spectators stayed well after the final whistle blew, honoring the coach who led the American squad to a 91-6-10 record. It was quite a feat for a coach who had stepped into a mess after the 2007 World Cup.

In the end, Pia Sundhage, the coach who had led the U.S. team to two Olympic gold medals and a second-place finish at the 2011 World Cup, didn't leave under a cloud of controversy and division. She simply got homesick and wanted to go back to Sweden. "I have been gone for so long and I want to go home," she said. "But I will miss this team. I am a much better coach than I was five years ago. This team has made me a better coach."

So amid tears and laughter she said her goodbyes, but not before the team gave her a guitar autographed in gold letters.

"It is the best gift I have ever gotten," she whispered.

She was on her way back to Sweden and the U.S. needed to find a new coach.

16

After Pia Sundhage announced her departure, the United States Soccer Federation immediately went into high gear searching high and low for the next coach. Getting it right was vital. Managing the U.S. National Team was one of the most visible jobs in the sport and it certainly wasn't the easiest. The committee in charge considered more than 30 candidates and finally determined that Tom Sermanni—a tough but affable Glasgow, Scotland, native—was the correct man for the difficult gig.

The new manager came from the Australian national team, where he led the Matildas into the top 10 in the world, but he also knew the American system, thanks to the three years he spent coaching the San Jose CyberRays and the New York Power of the Women's United Soccer Association.

Sermanni walked into a team that needed to transform into a more skilled and more tactical side. Sundhage had been very successful, but the players she had been coaching had been getting older and it seemed she had made few allowances for that. If the U.S. wanted to win the 2015 World Cup in Canada they would need to be more creative, smarter, and quicker. The rest of the world was catching up.

Despite the emergence of Alex Morgan as a brilliant scorer, Sermanni understood that he needed the most help in the midfield. Enter Tobin Heath and Lauren Holiday. The New Jersey-born Heath, an attacking midfielder by trade with a quiet disposition, was probably the most skilled player on the roster. She was another player Anson Dorrance had developed at UNC. She had a hippie-like free spirit and let-it-flow attitude. Dorrance thought she wouldn't survive her time at UNC because he always saw her on her skateboard bolting down the street of a large hill to get to class. One time, a car did hit her. Luckily, the only thing that broke was the skateboard. Perhaps learning to dodge cars on her skateboard had helped her, because where others saw walls of defenders, Heath saw a creative pass. She served as the link between a stout backline and the wonderful attacking forays of Morgan and Abby Wambach.

Lauren Holiday was a year older than Heath and was already a bit more established on the squad. She notched two goals and three assists during the 2011 World Cup, filling in nicely for 2012 Olympic hero Lloyd. The playmaking Indianapolis native possessed Heath's vision as well as a similar technical ability, although she seemed to get injured frequently. If Holiday could stay healthy and develop more chemistry with Heath, all Sermanni had to do was hand these two the keys to the powerful American engine and let them drive. They were ready.

Another newcomer was the brilliant, irrepressible Sydney Leroux. Although she grew up in Surrey, British Columbia, with a mom who played on the Canadian national softball team, the lightning-quick forward always dreamed of suiting up for the Stars and Stripes. Her father was an American who had a brief

baseball career. She got her first chance during the
CONCACAF qualifying game for the 2012 Olympics,
scoring an astonishing five goals in her second match.
She followed up that performance by becoming the
youngest member of the gold-medal winning side and
scoring a goal against New Zealand in the quarterfinals.
Unlike Heath and Cheney, Leroux's success wasn't
ensured, but she was well on her way.

Sermanni understood the task at hand. He needed
to mesh the growing talents of Heath, Holiday, Leroux,
and some of the other younger players, with the
established women who had brought home the gold
medal to America.

He had a tough job. This was a team that bled
legacy—they had two World Cup trophies and three
Olympic gold medals. They were also a team that was
consistently at the top of the world rankings. Countless
girls looked up to the achievements of the women in
the Red, White, and Blue and dreamed of becoming
the future Mia Hamm or Abby Wambach. He held
their dreams in his hands. But, most importantly, he
had to win.

And that is where he and the team fell short.

Sermanni attempted to rejuvenate the squad and succeeded at working younger players like Morgan Brian, Meghan Klingenberg, Julie Johnston, and Crystal Dunn into the starting lineup. But the goal of creating a cohesive vision, a playing style that combined the U.S.'s impressive athleticism with its improving tactical understanding and technical ability, never came together.

After a seventh-place finish at the 2014 Algarve Cup—by far the worst-ever showing from the Americans in the yearly tournament—Sermanni was unceremoniously fired. With the 2015 World Cup a little over a year away, the U.S. needed a new coach and some new answers.

17

Jill Ellis, like Michelle Akers, had played soccer with the boys when she was growing up. In 1970s England, where she was born, it was considered unladylike for girls to play soccer. So she would tag along with her brother and when the boys needed an extra player for a pickup game, she would join the fray. Ironically, in a land mad for soccer, she would not get to play organized soccer until her family moved to the United States. Her father was a soccer coach and decided to bring his knowledge of the game to the States. She was fourteen years old and gravitated to soccer because she was a shy newcomer and found that she could make friends playing sports.

Ellis got good enough to earn a scholarship at William and Mary and was named third-team all-American three years running. But, in 1985 with no national team yet and no women's professional league, she had run into the same soccer wall that all women at that time hit: she needed a job because soccer was considered a hobby. However, soccer was in her blood and even though she had earned a master's degree in technical writing and had a decent job, she was bored.

In 1994, when April Heinrichs offered her a coaching assistant job at the University of Maryland for far less money than she was making at her job, she didn't hesitate: she said yes. Later, when she was asked to start the women's soccer program at the University of Illinois, she jumped at it. Two years later, she was head coach at UCLA. In her second year as coach there, she was named national coach of the year.

Ellis had worked extensively with the USSF's youth program and was an assistant coach under Pia Sundhage for the 2008 Olympics and the 2011 World Cup. Afterwards she was named the United States Soccer Federation's development director for women's programs. When Sundhage stepped down, she was named interim coach and was considered a logical choice for the head coaching job. But she turned it down then, saying she needed to spend more time with her family. After the firing of Tom Sermanni, however, she had a change of heart and said yes when the job was offered to her again. Jill Ellis wasn't a big name when she took over the head coaching job on May 16, 2014. She was an insider who the players knew very well and she was respected in the inner circles of the USSF, but most people's reactions outside of soccer circles was, "Jill Who?"

Ellis knew that the world was catching up in terms of skill and the quality of their programs. Coaching the U.S. team in the early days had been easier when the United States had a clear advantage over other countries regarding women athletes who had been trained in quality college soccer programs. That was no longer the case. Ellis understood that she had been hired to bring the World Cup trophy back to the U.S. It had been sixteen years since the U.S. team last hoisted it above their victorious heads and they wanted it back.

During her first meeting with the team, she made it clear what her coaching philosophy was by placing a quote on the team blackboard that stated, "Even if you are on the right track, if you sit still, you'll get run over."

She didn't have a lot of time to get the team ready, but her familiarity with the players helped. Megan Rapinoe felt that the familiarity Ellis already had with the team before she was named head coach really helped. "She has a good rapport with the players off the field and that allows her to give criticism and say it like it is. We have a pretty honest relationship with her."

But there were still some lingering doubts among others whether Ellis was the right person to take over the job. Retired legend Michelle Akers, for one, thought that Ellis was a "nice person," but made it no secret that she thought her old coach, Tony DiCicco should have gotten the nod. Others pointed out that Ellis had led UCLA to eight NCAA Women's Soccer Cup finals and did not win once. On the national stage, her Under-20 team was ousted by Nigeria in the quarterfinals of the 2010 Under-20 World Cup.

She wasn't as flamboyant or outspoken as Sundhage or even Serminni. She was quiet and analytical. Did she really have what it took to deal with some very strong personalities on the team and lead the U.S. to that elusive World Cup trophy?

18

Carli Lloyd had been putting up with criticisms about her play for about as long as she could remember. She readily admitted that as a young player, while talented, she didn't concentrate on fitness and training as much as she should have. Her raw talent saw her through. Many people were baffled by Lloyd. She was a player who had scored the winning goals in not one, but two, Olympic Gold medal games. But there were times when the U.S. midfielder looked like she didn't belong on the field with the rest of the players. She would make mistakes, giving the ball up easily and handing opponents easy scoring opportunities. Often she would take ill-advised shots on goal when other teammates were open and had better looks.

Pia Sundhage had actually benched her for the 2012 Olympics, concerned that Lloyd's mistakes on the field would hurt the team. When Shannon Boxx went out with an injury in the first game, Lloyd came in and was instrumental in leading the U.S. to victory in that match. Her inspired play in the next five games led the U.S. to a gold medal. She scored the winning goal in the gold-medal match.

Lloyd was an old-school American player in the Wambach and Akers mold who relied on her physicality and athleticism to get her through. As she got older, she trained harder. She was a fierce competitor who liked proving the doubters wrong. She had come up big in too many important games to count her out. But there were nagging doubts about her consistency. She could be both brilliant and weak in the same game.

So where exactly would she fit in Ellis's new scheme of creativity, skill, and ball possession? And more importantly, which Carli Lloyd would show up at the 2015 World Cup?

While some were questioning what Carli Lloyd

would do in the 2015 World Cup, others were openly talking about the aging Abby Wambach and what her future might hold. The woman who had bested Mia Hamm's seemingly unbreakable international goal record and had accomplished nearly everything in the world of soccer during her long career had never won a World Cup title. She would be thirty-five years old for the 2015 World Cup. If the U.S. didn't win it this time, it was highly unlikely that Wambach would be around for the next one four years later. It seemed unfair that arguably the best female soccer player to set foot on the planet would have to walk away from her storied career without a World Cup title under her belt.

Wambach wanted it badly. After she won her second Olympic Gold medal in 2012, she turned to her partner and said, "Well, this is great. But I want to win a World Cup."

There was no doubt that she and the team were serious about bringing that trophy home.

During the 2014 CONCACAF Championship that doubled as a World Cup qualifying tournament, the U.S. went on a tear. After an initial falter against Trinidad and Tobago in which they squeezed out a 1-0 win, the team went on to destroy the rest of the field to win the championship. Abby Wambach showed she had plenty left in the tank, scoring seven goals and winning the Golden Boot for the most goals scored. The critics of Carli Lloyd were silenced momentarily when she won the Golden Ball for best player in the tournament.

The rest of 2014 and early 2015 didn't go without setbacks. A very good French squad beat the U.S. 2-0, putting the team on notice that they would be facing stiff World Cup competition. However, they later turned the tables, beating the French to win the 2015 Algarve Cup. A couple of the new "kids," Julie Johnson and Christen Press, looked particularly impressive.

Going into the 2015 World Cup, there were questions about the U.S. squad. Hope Solo was involved in some off-field legal issues. Would that distraction prove harmful? Alex Morgan had suffered a serious bone bruise on her knee and had not played for the U.S. squad since April. Would she be ready to see action in time for the Cup? Abby Wambach had not been a starter in the last nine games. Would Ellis turn more to the veteran during the tournament?

They drew a difficult group, termed the Group of Death or the Group of Extreme Exhaustion. The U.S. would face Nigeria, Sweden, now led by former U.S. coach Pia Sundhage, and a much-improved Australian squad.

In their first match against Australia at Winnipeg Stadium, the U.S. found out how difficult the group would be. The Australians fought hard, but the Americans, led by Megan Rapinoe with two goals, outlasted the Matildas. After the 3-1 victory, Rapinoe admitted, "It was a bit of a shaky game for us, especially the first 30 minutes. But three points. That's what is most important."

In the next game against their favorite singing coach's team, the U.S. drew with Sweden, 0-0. In the final game against Nigeria, Wambach, who had not gotten the start in the first two group games, got the starting nod. She repaid Ellis's faith by scoring her 183rd international and game-winning goal. Ellis said, "I just know Abby, I know big moments, I know she will deliver. I'm really pleased with the investment tonight."

The U.S. won Group D, but they did not have a

signature game in which they had dominated. While their defense was solid, allowing only one goal, the offense looked lost. They were set to face a scrappy Columbia in the round of 16. Before the game, Columbian star, Lady Andrade, threw down the gauntlet, saying, "The U.S. thinks we're a team they are going to walk all over and it will be an easy game for them. We're going to beat them since they like to talk so much."

The U.S. didn't counter her statement, preferring to do their "talking" on the field. But it was another lackluster performance. Although the strong backline shut down Lady Andrade and the Columbian goalie was ejected, forcing the Columbians to play short-handed, the U.S. looked like the old U.S. team that relied more on athleticism than creativity. The 2-0 victory over Colombia was not pretty. But Jill Ellis said that she would take an ugly World Cup victory over defeat, adding, "I'm pleased with where we are."

Others were less than pleased with where the U.S. squad was at. Fans and commentators were openly criticizing Ellis's tactics. Michelle Akers' words were perhaps the most stinging: "We don't have all of our pieces together, we aren't performing at our best, and some of our coaching decisions are unexplainable."

It seemed that the only offensive tactic the team had in its arsenal was to feed the ball to Wambach for a header. They would have to do much better if they were going to get by China in the quarterfinals.

They did play better against China. Forced to play without Rapinoe and Lauren Holiday due to accumulated yellow card ejections, the U.S. had to rework their starting lineup. Ellis made a decision to free up Carli Loyd to play more of an attacking midfielder role.

It turned out to be a brilliant stroke by Ellis. Lloyd, who had been quiet in the offense up to this point, scored the winning goal against the Chinese. Although, the score was just 1-0, the United States thoroughly dominated the match on both ends of the field. It looked like the team was finally starting to put the pieces together. It still remained to be seen if they would have all pistons firing when they faced the number one team in the world in the semifinals.

The Germans were the new face of women's soccer. They were quick, skilled, and creative. Forwards Anja Mittag and Célia Šašić were the most dangerous attacking duo in the world. Couple that force with the goalkeeping prowess of former FIFA Player of the Year, Angela Angerer, and it was little wonder the United States had lost its number-one ranking to this young and talented German squad.

The U.S., buoyed by their exceptional game against China in the quarterfinals, was not intimidated. Ellis moved Wambach back to the bench, starting Alex Morgan and Lloyd, a gamble that worked as the Red, White, and Blue connected passes, enjoyed long spells of possession, and created plenty of chances in the first half. But Angerer proved time and again why she was one of the top goalies in the world and the Americans came up empty in the first half. The score was tied 0-0. The game outcome was almost determined in the second half, when Julie Johnson, who had played brilliant defense during the entire tournament, dragged Alexandra Popp down in the box in the 59th minute for a penalty kick. But Šašić, perhaps intimidated by the moment, missed the penalty kick well to the left.

About ten minutes later, the U.S. would have its chance to bury a penalty kick, when the referee blew the whistle for a foul against Morgan inside the box. It was a controversial call, as it looked like Morgan had been fouled just outside of the box. But the call was made and could not be taken back. Carli Lloyd buried the kick, giving the U.S. a 1-0 lead. The Americans added an insurance goal 15 minutes later, when Kelley O'Hara, on an assist from Lloyd, volleyed home the second goal of the night.

When the final whistle blew, the Americans had done it. They had won 2-0 and were going to the final! Naysayers who had been criticizing Ellis's tactics and roster decisions had changed their minds. Suddenly, the maligned coach was a genius who had led the United States back where it belonged!

It appeared the U.S. was peaking at the right time. But there was still business to attend to. "We didn't come here to just make the final," Lloyd said. "We came here to win it."

19

Earlier in the month, Abby Wambach made the announcement that the 2015 World Cup would be her last. If she was going to add the crown jewel of a World Cup championship to her exceptional career, this would be her last chance. Carli Lloyd vowed, "For this being her last one, I will do whatever it takes to get the job done."

It would also be the last chance for team captain, Christie Rampone, to pick up another World Cup championship. The shy 40-year-old defender was the last player left from the 1999 U.S. team that had won the World Cup. It seemed appropriate that she should start and end her career hoisting the trophy.

Once again, the U.S. was going to face Japan in the finals, and both the Japanese and the Americans had some scores to settle. The U.S. was seeking revenge for their heartbreaking 2011 World Cup loss, and Japan was looking to even the score for their loss to the Americans in the 2012 Olympic gold medal match. The Japanese were also motivated to send off one of their veterans with a World Cup trophy. Homare Sawa, the Japanese star and team leader who had led the Japanese to their first-ever World Cup championship in 2011, was appearing in her last Cup. At thirty-seven years old, she had appeared in a record six World Cup tournaments. She had been the twenty-year-old captain of the Japanese team the last time the U.S. had won the World Cup.

It would be an interesting match. The U.S., which had only allowed one goal in the entire tournament would be facing a well-balanced opponent famous for its passing and patience.

Everybody expected a low scoring match. What actually happened on July 5, 2015 took the world by complete surprise.

Within the first 16 minutes of the final, the match

was virtually over. In the third minute, Lloyd sprinted towards a Rapinoe corner kick—a play drawn up by Ellis during training—and she finished past helpless defender Kaihori. Two minutes later, with Japan still reeling, Lloyd scored again as another free kick found its way to her feet and she side-footed the ball into the net. In the 14th minute, a poor Japanese clearance gifted Holiday an opportunity inside the box and she volleyed home the third. Then Lloyd iced the game with her dagger from midfield two minutes later. Japan was down 4-0 before the two teams had even broken a sweat at BC Place in Vancouver.

To their credit, the Japanese never gave up. They would score two, although one of those scores was an own goal by Julie Johnson on an errant header. When Tobin Heath scored America's fifth goal in the second half, it was obvious that there would be no comeback for the Japanese.

Wambach hadn't started the game, but in a gesture of respect and legacy, Ellis put her in the match late in the second half. The crowd erupted as Carli Lloyd showed the superstar leader deference by taking off her blue captain armband and giving it to Wambach.

Ellis also put team captain, Christie Rampone, in the game. When the veteran defender stepped onto the field, at 40 years-old and 11 days, she officially became the oldest player ever to play in a woman's World Cup match. The two veterans would get their title and they would get it contributing to the team on the field.

When the final whistle finally blew, the decidedly pro-American crowd erupted into deafening chants of "U-S-A! U-S-A!"

The American squad went wild, hugging each other and jumping up and down. Then as a team they did a victory lap around the field as the crowd screamed its approval. They had done it. They had become the first team to win three women's World Cup Championships and they had done it in convincing fashion. The 16-year drought was officially over.

Overcome with emotion, Abby Wambach ran to the stands and kissed her wife. It was an image that would makes its rounds across the globe. Carli Lloyd was on her knees, hugging teammates. She had made history today, having the fastest hat trick in women's World Cup history. She would go on to win the Golden Ball for the best player of the tournament. Given her performance in the final, it was never in doubt.

Hope Solo would take home the Golden Glove.

The victory was vindication for Coach Jill Ellis, who had been roundly criticized at the beginning of the tournament for her team's lackluster play. "Did I envision winning?" she said. "Yes. Did I envision lifting a trophy with five goals? That was a dream come true. Pinch me. Wake me up!"

When the team finally hoisted the trophy, the women were all smiles. It had been a long, sometimes difficult, and lonely road, but they had finally arrived at their destination. They had brought the World Cup championship back home where it belonged.

20

The team rode on red, white, and blue floats while ticker tape and confetti streamed on them. They hoisted the World Cup trophy as throngs of people lined the streets along the Canyon of Heroes and cheered them on from Battery Park to City Hall in New York City. The mayor of New York had called the U.S. Women's National Soccer team heroines on and off the field and he felt that America's Heroes deserved a ticker tape parade. Although individual women athletes had been given parades before, it would be the first women's team in American history so honored.

The crowd was filled with fans, both young and old,

who had come to celebrate their accomplishments and to pay tribute to America's returning heroes. And surely, there were more than a few little girls in the throng with stars in their eyes, dreaming they might be standing in the sunlight one day and hoisting the trophy. A 14-year-old girl from New Jersey, Carli Lloyd's home state, told reporters, "Women from sports dominated by men are finally getting the attention they need. It's inspiring to young girls."

At a massive rally held at City Hall, Mayor Bill DeBlasio handed each of the players a key to the city and said, "Young women who watched that game will grow up and they'll tell their daughters and they'll tell their sons about that 2015 championship team that made history—and opened our minds and brought us together."

When asked to speak at the rally, Abby Wambach thanked the fans. "I can't discount how important you guys were—the fans—in bringing home this World Cup for us," she said. "We've had a lot of amazing experiences... but this actually will go down as the best thing I have ever been a part of in my life."

It was a far cry from a mere 24 years ago, when the

returning 1991 world champions returned to John F. Kennedy Airport to a welcoming crowd of three people. But, women's soccer had come a long way since then.

This American team could stand on the shoulders of giants like Michelle Akers, Mia Hamm, Julie Foudy, Christine Lilly, Brandi Chastain, and many others; women who had to fight to get the respect the women's soccer team deserved. The first squad had played for the love of the game, getting paid next to nothing and competing in empty stadiums while being ignored by the media even though they were the best in the world.

As time went on, the women's team forced their way into the spotlight through hard work and sheer determination. They were distinctly American: they knew Americans love winners and they loved to win.

As the 2015 women's national soccer team basked in the love and cheers from the crowd in New York, the mayor reminded the rally that this had been the first ticker tape parade for any women's team, ever.

"It's about time, isn't it?" he proclaimed.

To all the women soccer players over the past

30 years who had sacrificed everything to become champions on and off the field, it wasn't about time.

It was long overdue.

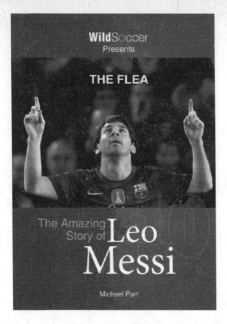

The Flea – The Amazing Story of Leo Messi

By Michael Part

The captivating story of soccer legend Lionel Messi, from his first touch at age five in the streets of Rosario, Argentina, to his first goal on the Camp Nou pitch in Barcelona, Spain. *The Flea* tells the amazing story of a boy who was born to play the beautiful game and destined to become the world's greatest soccer player. The best-selling book by Michael Part is a must read for every soccer fan!

Ages 9 and up

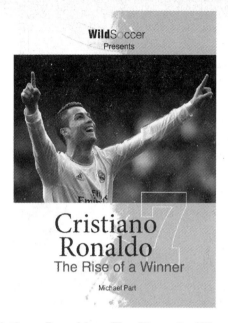

WildSoccer
Presents

Cristiano
Ronaldo
The Rise of a Winner

Michael Part

Cristiano Ronaldo – The Rise of a Winner

By Michael Part

Cristiano Ronaldo: The Rise of a Winner is the gripping life story of a boy who rose from the streets of Madeira to become one of the greatest soccer players ever. This heartfelt, stirring tale chronicles Ronaldo's road to glory, a journey that made him the man he is today.

Michael Part is the author of *The Flea: The Amazing Story of Leo Messi, The Pope Who Loves Soccer,* and the Disney classic *A Kid in King Arthur's Court.*

Ages 9 and up

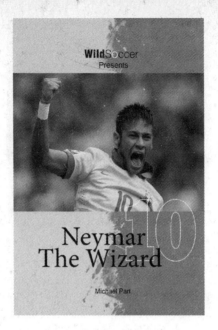

Neymar The Wizard

By Michael Part

Neymar The Wizard is the fascinating coming of age story of Neymar Junior, the skinny kid from Mogi Das Cruzes in Brazil, who has been called the next Pelé. Neymar has taken Brazil and the world by storm and continues to inspire millions around the world with his talent, his open heart, and his engaging smile. Following the international bestsellers, *The Flea: The Amazing Story of Leo Messi* and *Ronaldo, The Rise of a Winner* by Michael Part, *Neymar The Wizard* is a heartwarming and emotional story about a father and son who, against all odds, made the journey from the verge of poverty to international stardom through love, conviction, and belief.

Michael Part is also the critically acclaimed author of *The Pope Who Loves Soccer,* the first account on Pope Francis coming of age and his lifelong love to soccer.

Ages 9 and up

Balotelli – The Untold Story

By Michael Part

Talented, unique, and always on the edge, this is the story of *Mario Balotelli's* journey from near death as an infant to becoming one of the world's best known strikers. Balotelli's story is one of triumph over personal and racial challenges, and his struggle to find his own true identity.

Michael Part is the best-selling author of *The Flea - The Amazing Story of Leo Messi, Cristiano Ronaldo - the Rise of a Winner, Neymar - The Wizard,* and *The Pope Who Loves Soccer.* His books are published in more than 30 countries worldwide.

Ages 9 and up